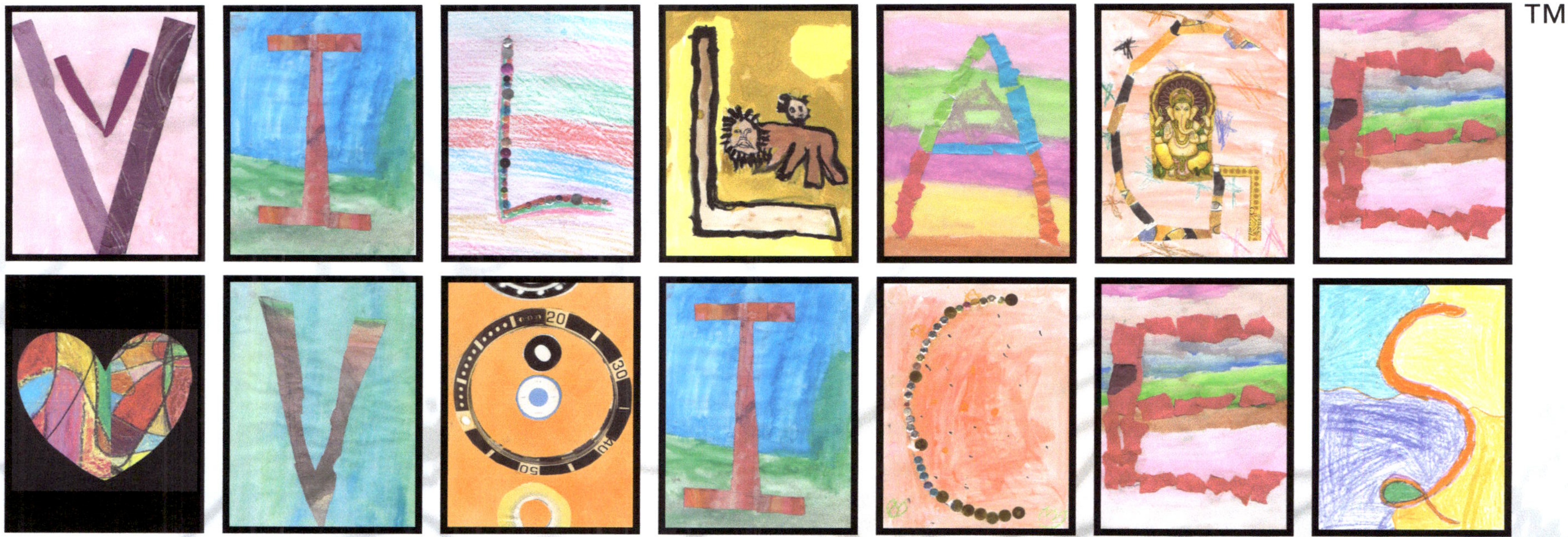

TM

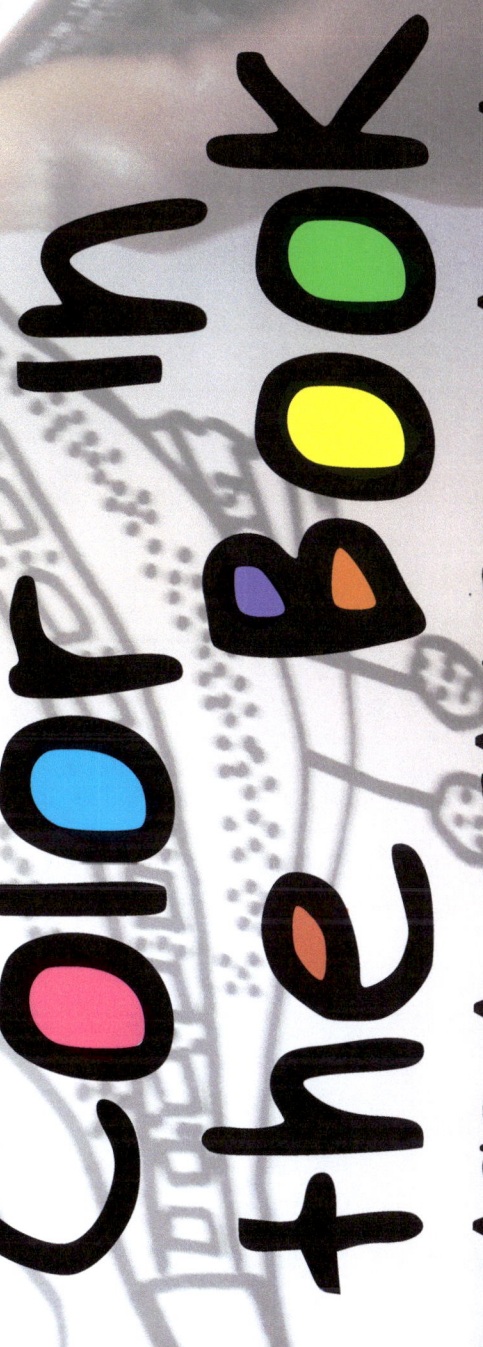

BOOKS BY KIDS, FOR KIDS

Color in the Book

INTERNATIONAL CREATIVE COLLABORATION

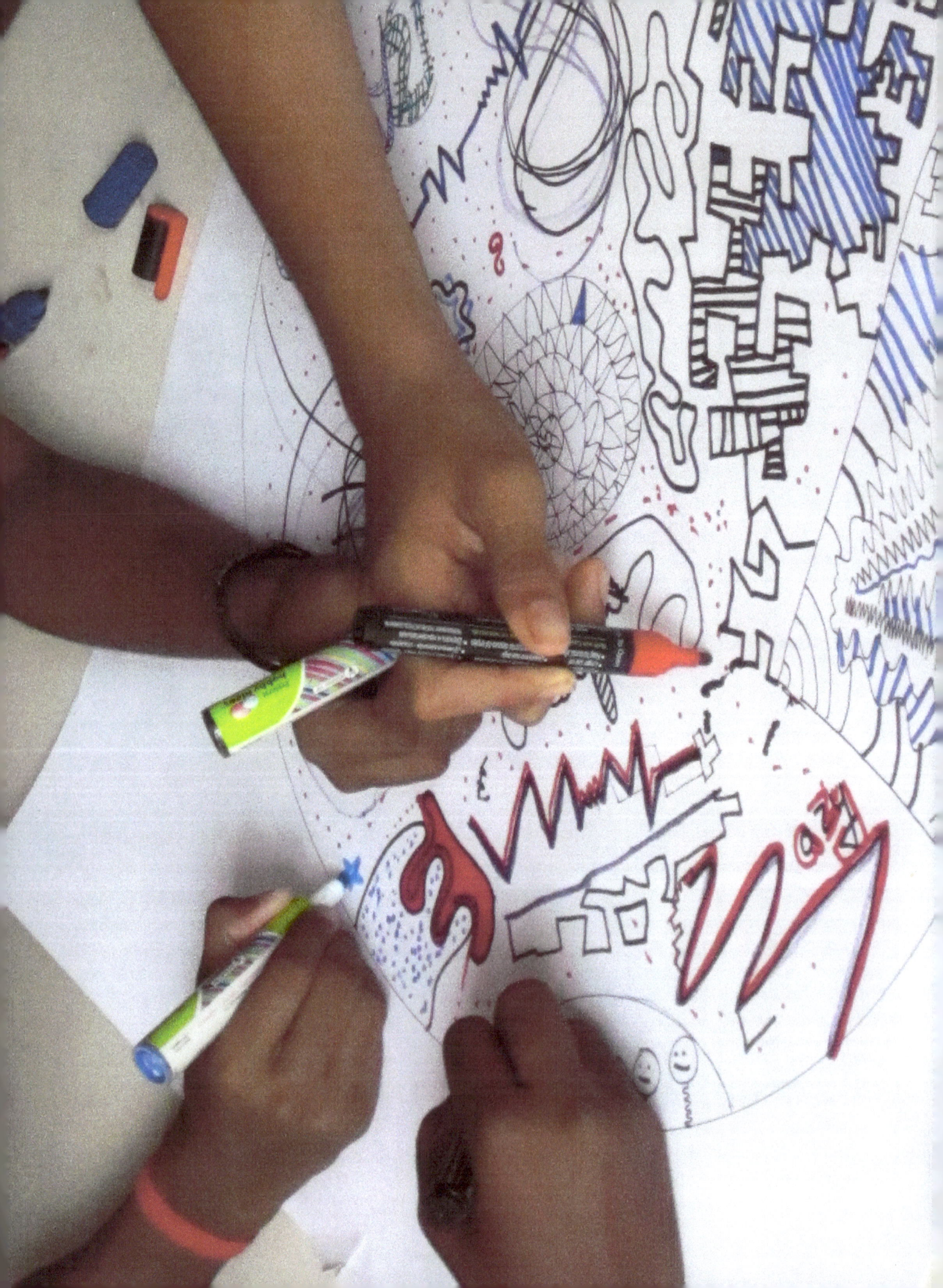

NEW MOON BOOKS
is an imprint of Salt River Publishing
Phoenix, Arizona
www.SaltRiverPublishing.com

First edition 2016
18 17 16   3 2 1   iii ii i
ISBN: 978-1535582780

Cover art by students in South India
Art editing by Kartik Gera

Publisher discount available
SaltRiverPublishing.com/estore/

Art Therapy (Integral Art) provides a VOICE where one may or may not exist...

I dedicate VILLAGE VOICES to children of all ages... May they be blessed with a voice, a vision, the divine light of creativity, self-expression, a love of books and reading.

"Never forget the goal.
Never stop aspiring.
Never halt in your progress, and you will succeed."

The Mother

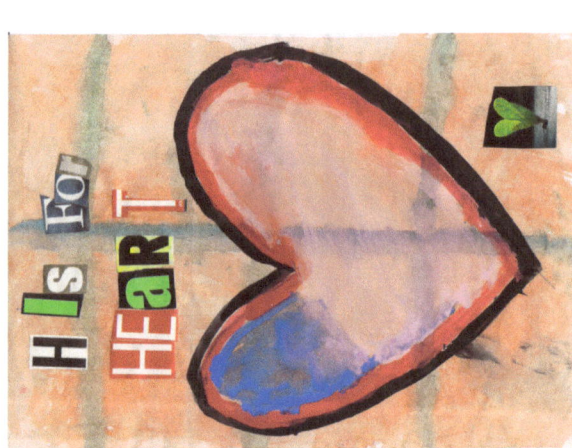

TIA PLEIMAN

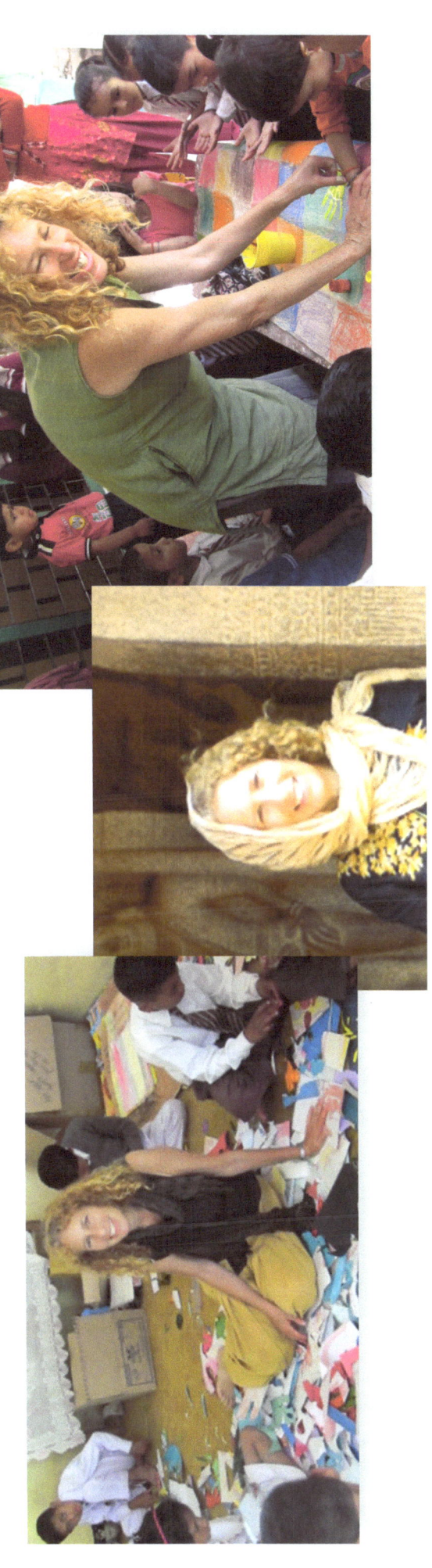

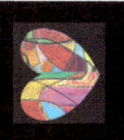

"Village Voices" is a series of books created by village children of all ages. The focus is on Art and Literacy – the result is creative empowerment. The intention of Village Voices is to nurture creativity and self-expression and to inspire a joy for reading.

The project and programs are facilitated by Tia Pleiman, MA, an international art therapist from the USA with 25 years of art therapy and educational experience. For the past 8 years, Tia has been working with urban and village children in north and south India and Nepal.

Tia is passionately committed to facilitating personal growth and development of children, youth and adults through Art Therapy. The tools of transformation are: The philosophies and practice of Integral Education combined with Art Therapy (Integral Art), which serve as the foundation for social, emotional and intellectual development through creative expression, self-reflection, literacy and peace building skills on both an individual and collective level.

THANK YOU for purchasing Village Voices, books by kids for kids. You are helping to support Create and Transform, providing community-based, grassroots Art and Literacy programs and projects, as well as the young authors, artists and schools they attend.

Facebook: Art Therapy with Create and Transform
www.createandtransform.org
tialovesart@gmail.com

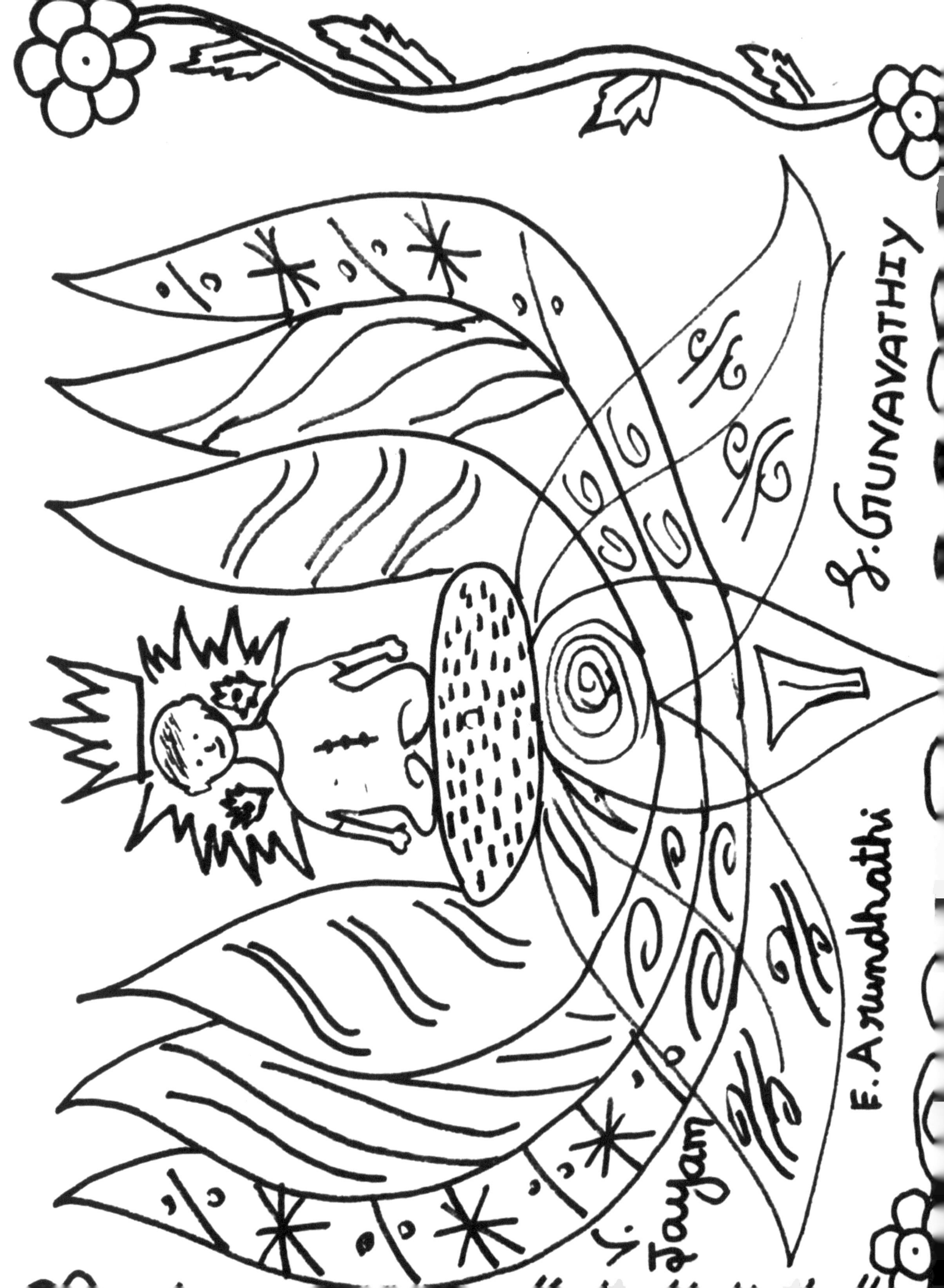

S. GUNAVATHIY

E. Arundhathi

In my dream I see fish.

And I runaway and I see fish.

by Anil

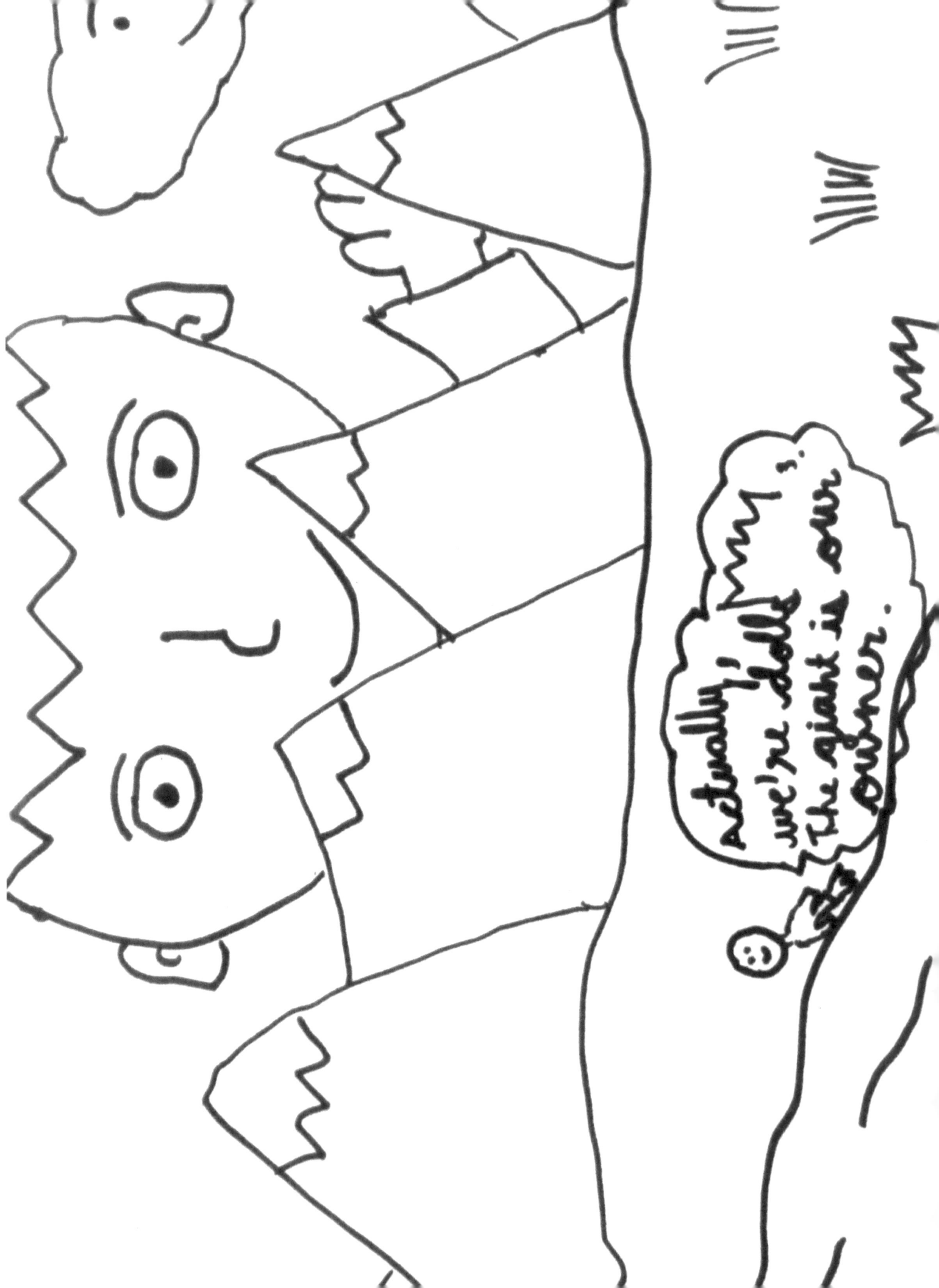

WHEN I GROW UP I WANT TO BE A

doctor in a hospital

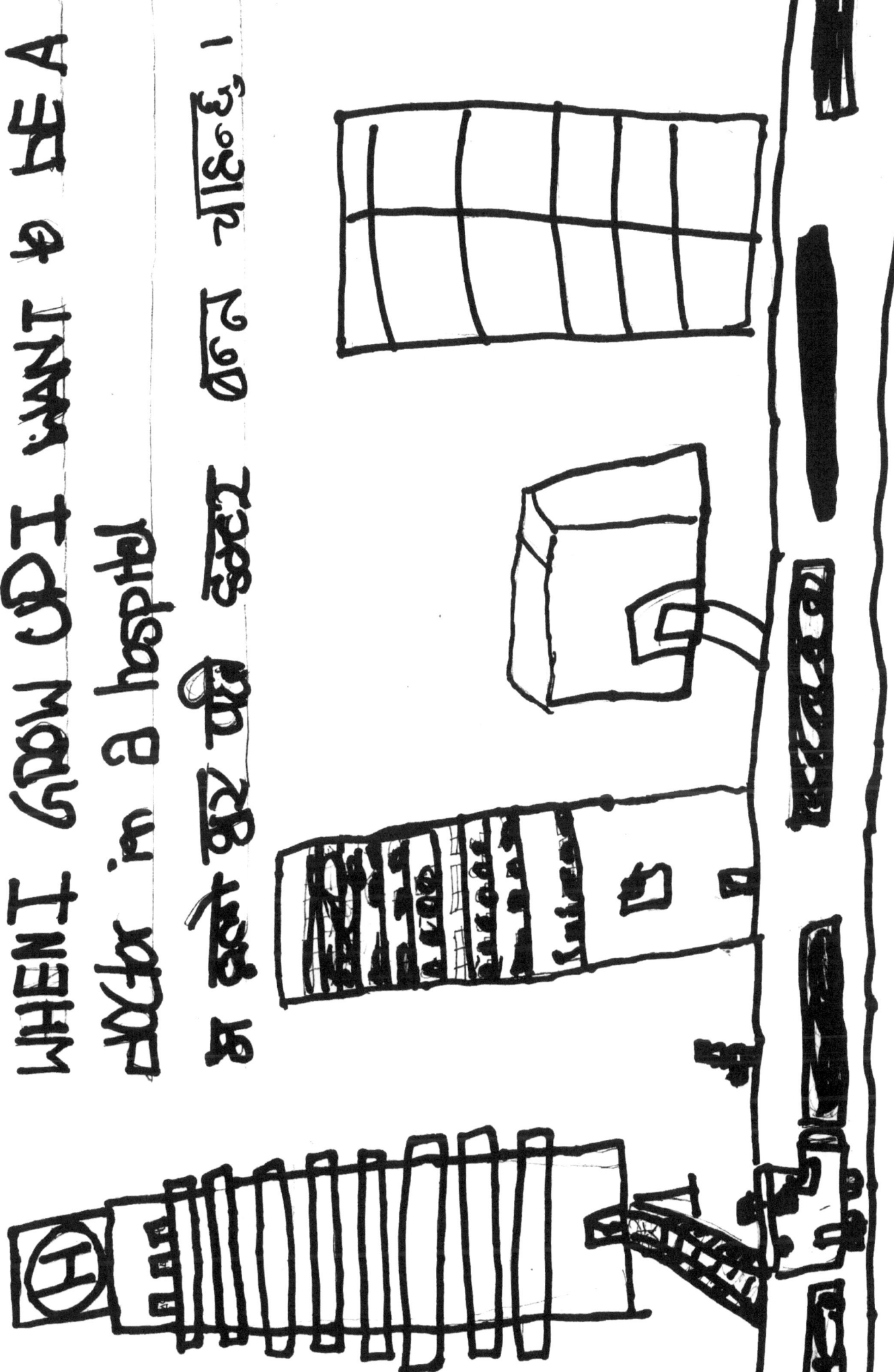

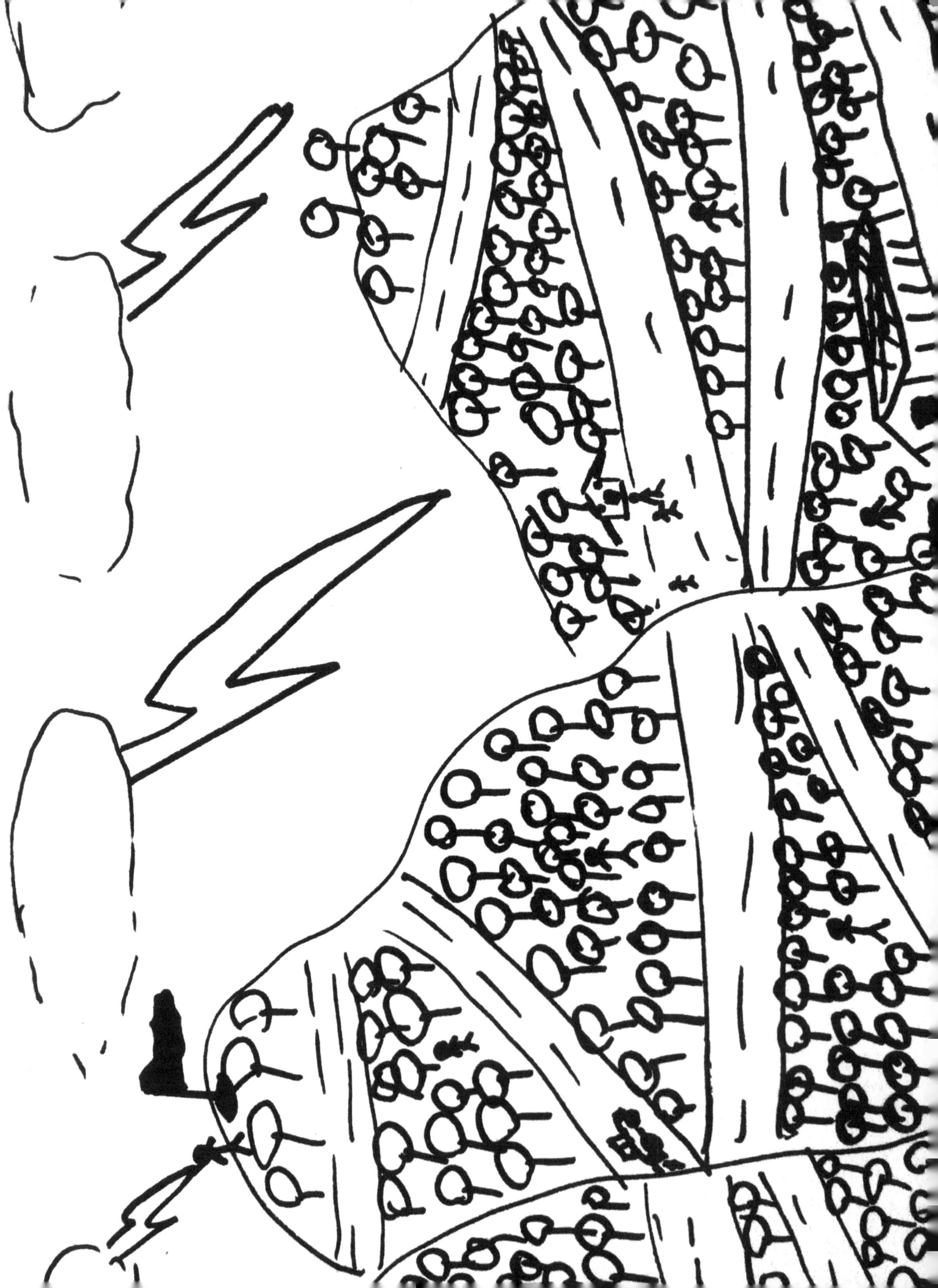

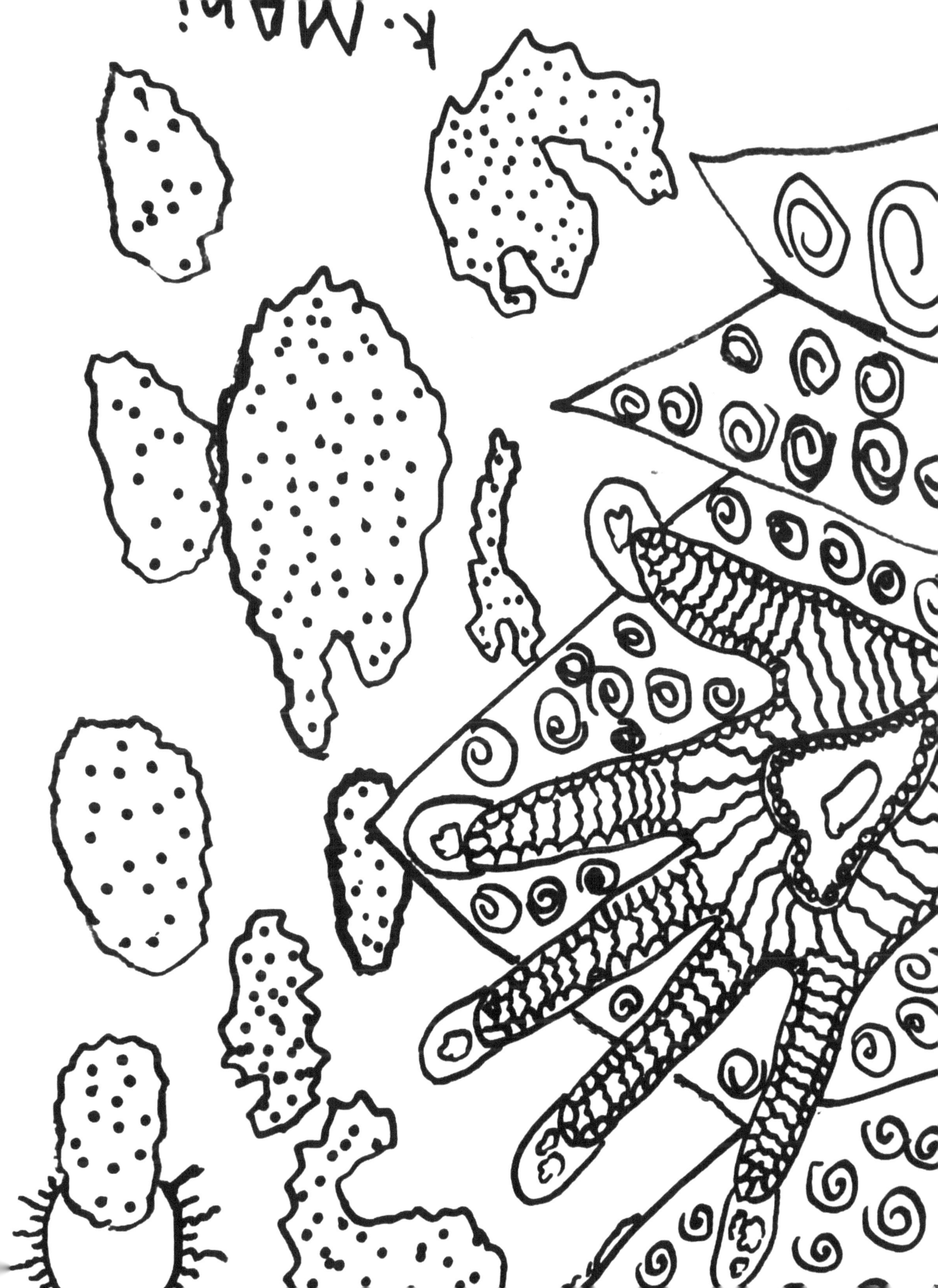

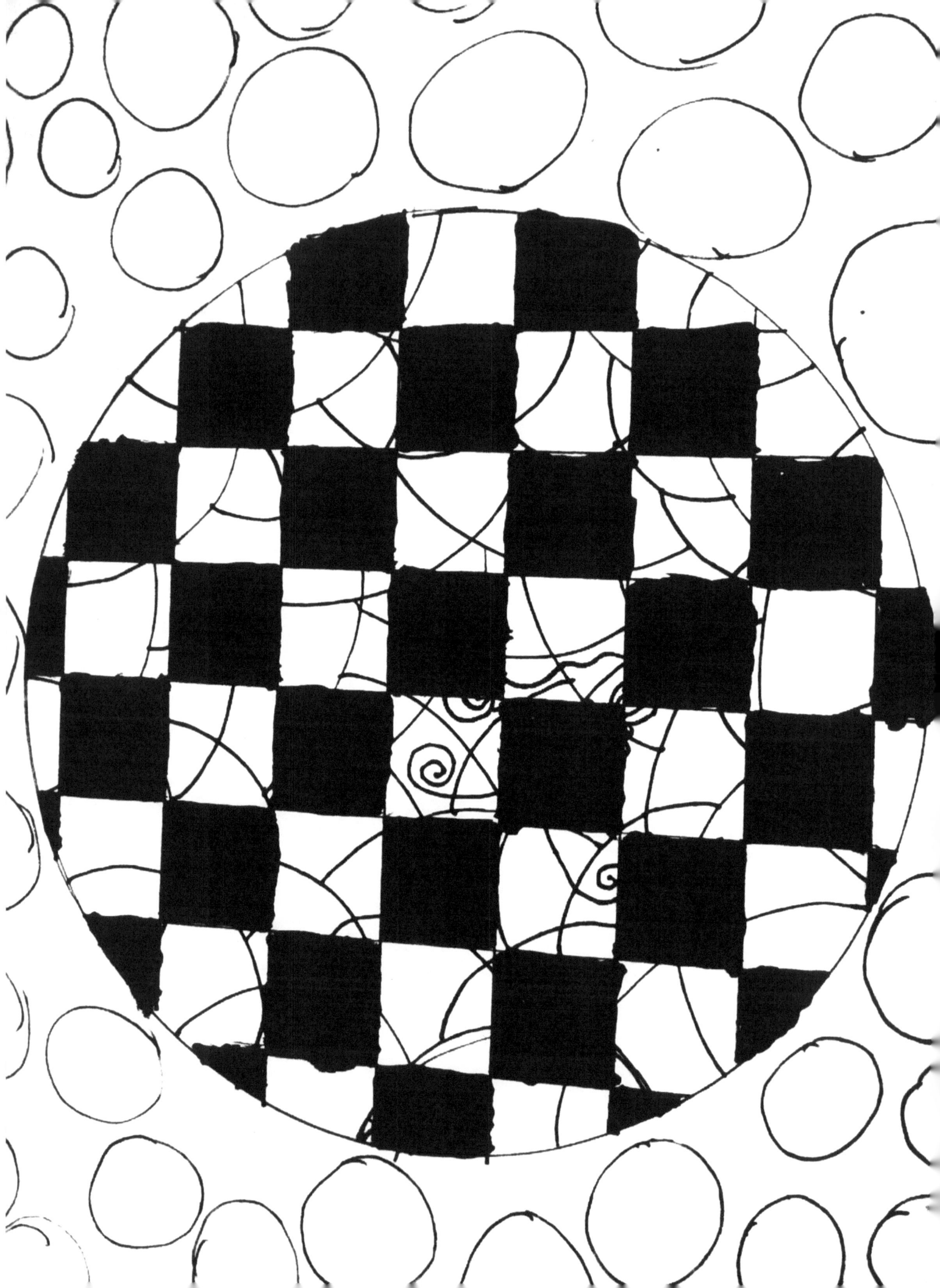

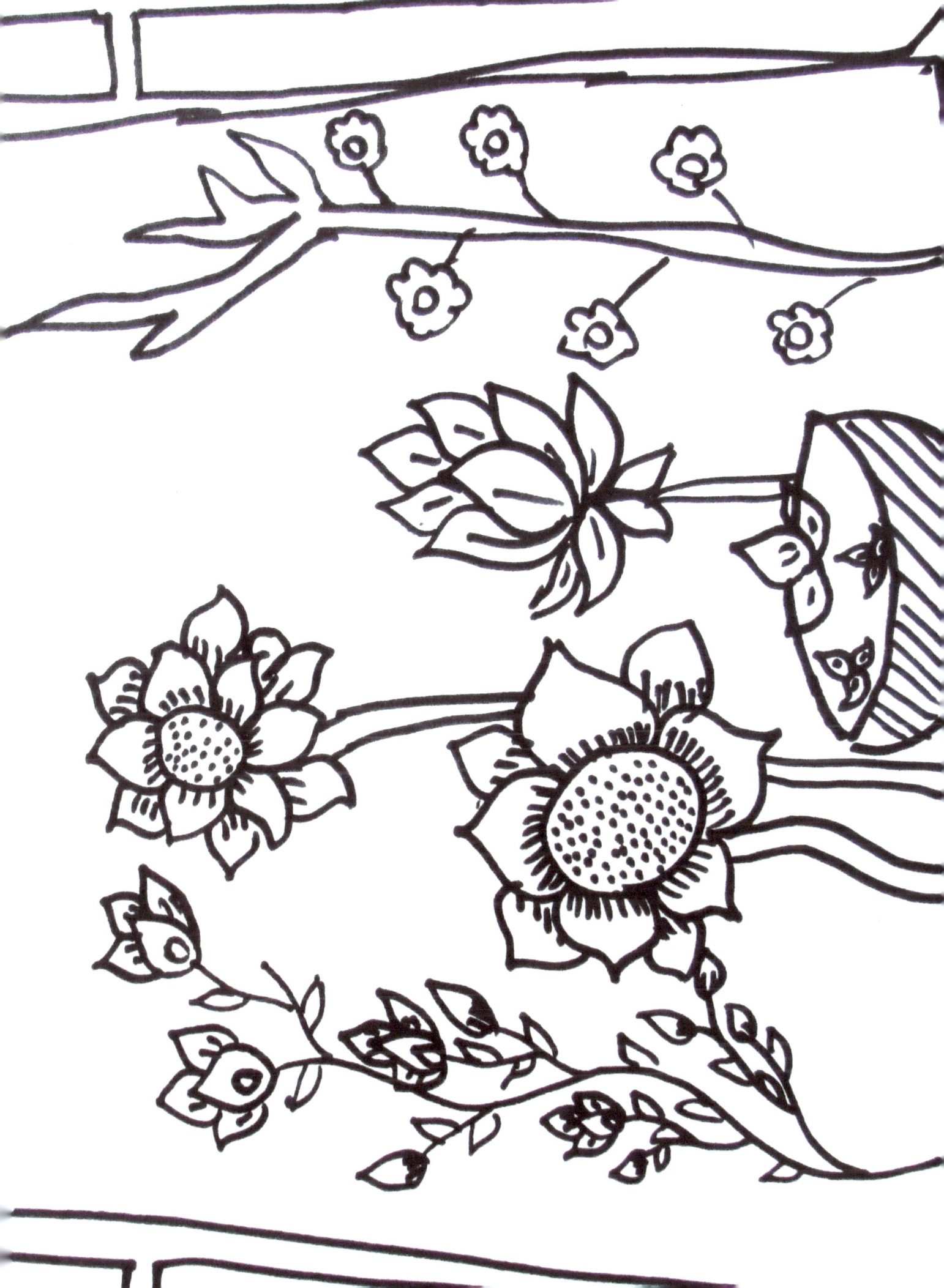

I feel happy when I eat
food. मैं जब खाता
हूँ।

I feel happy when I eat
आनंद

स्वाद

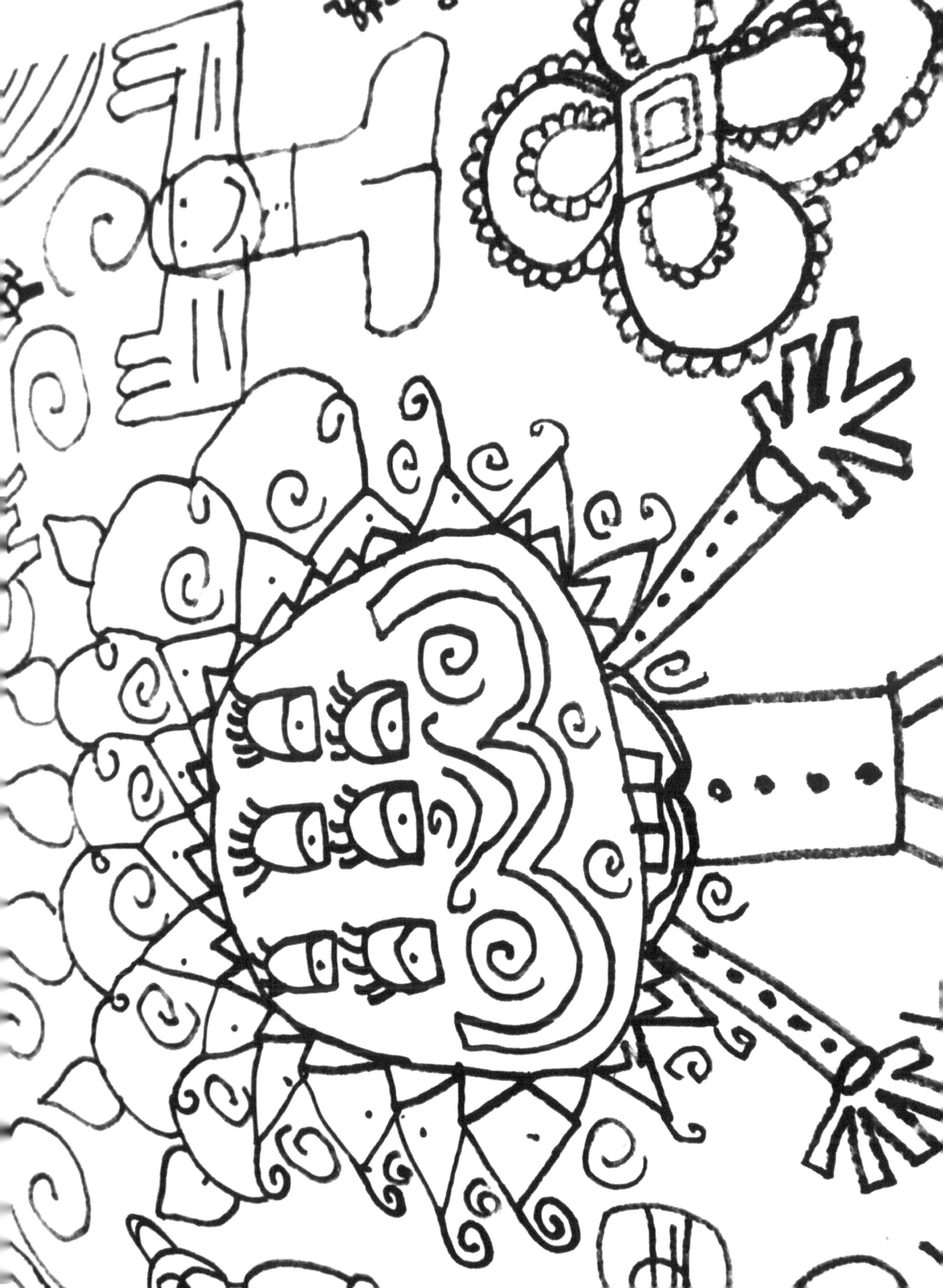

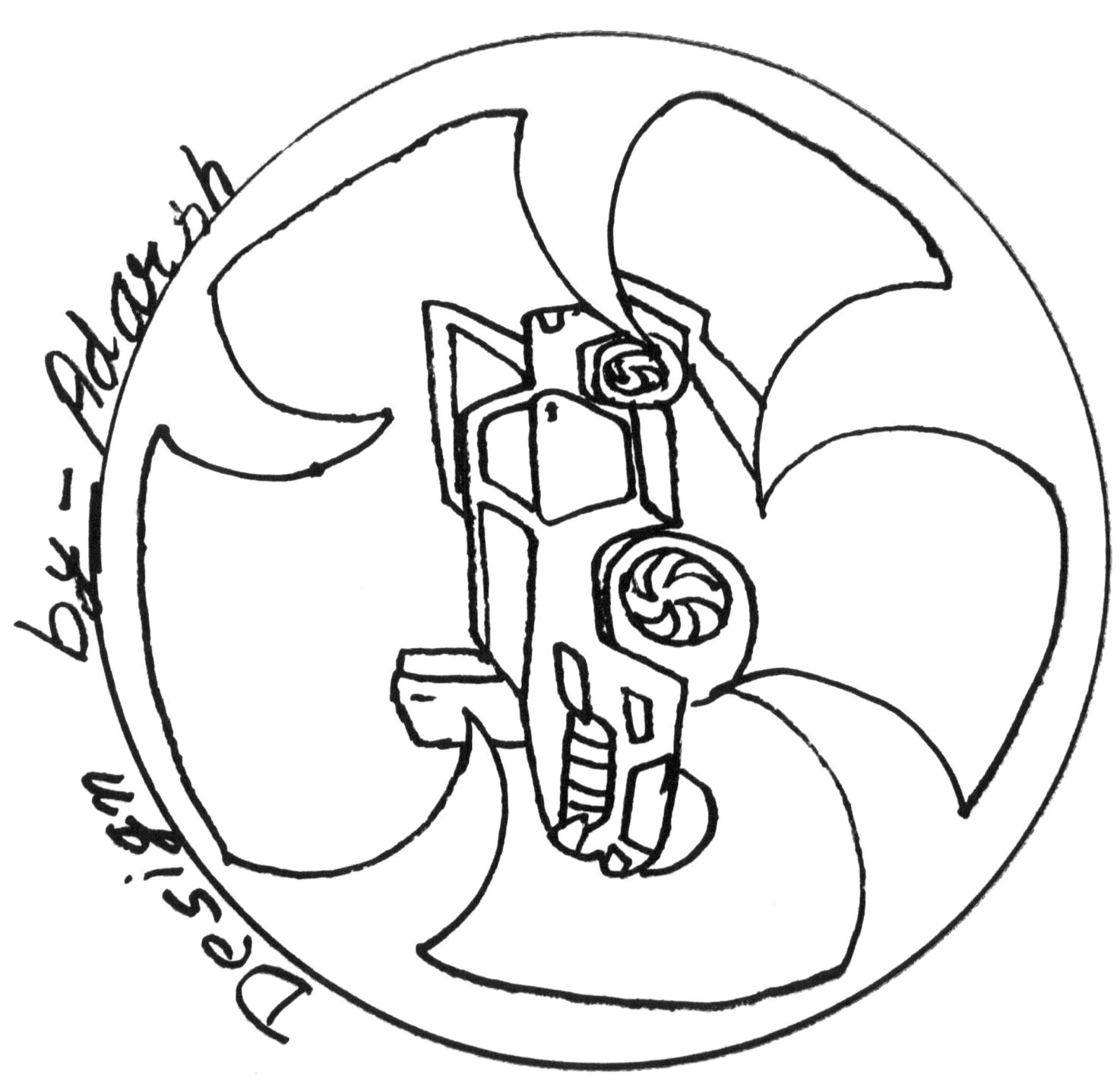

by - Adarsh

Design

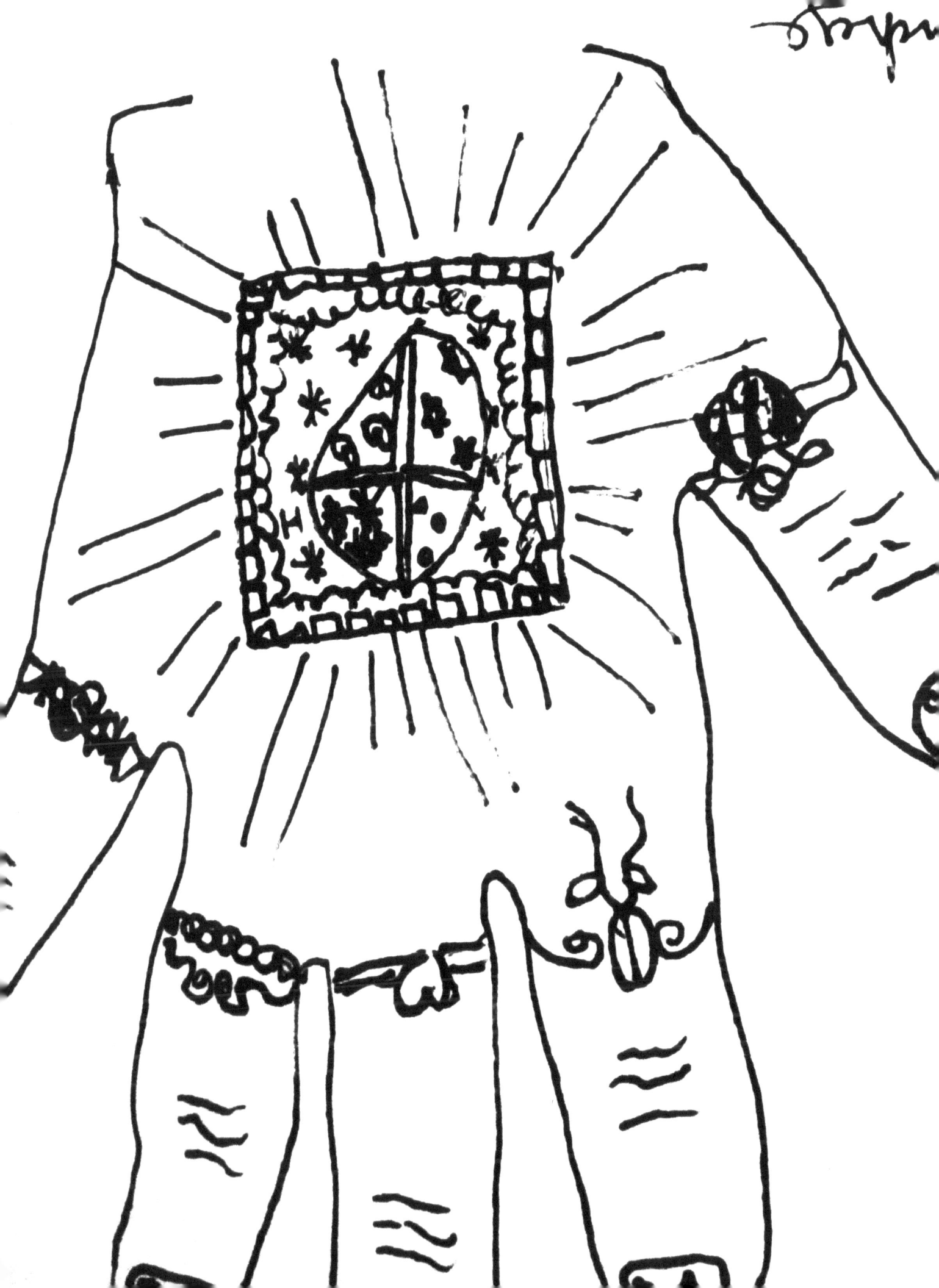

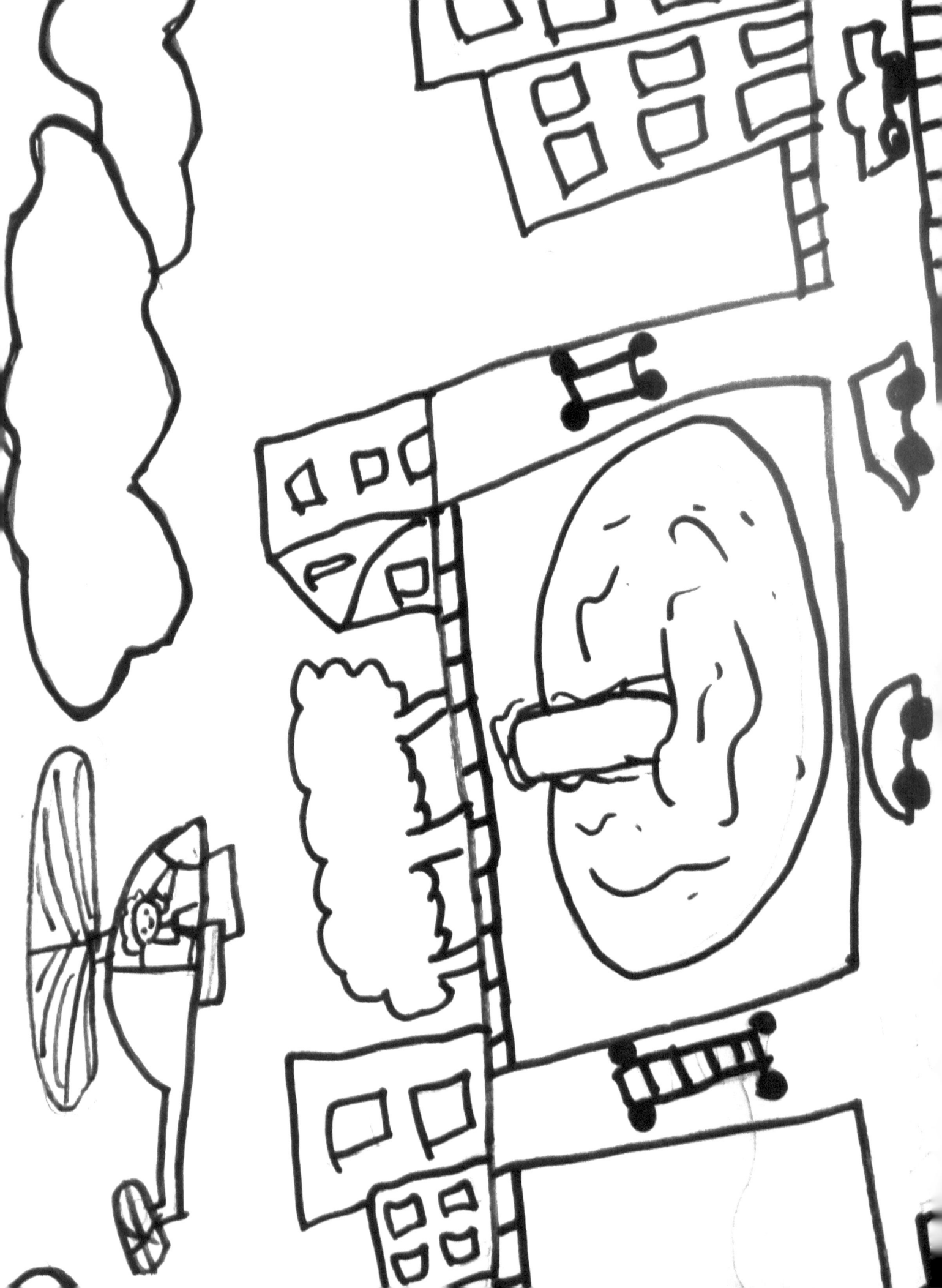

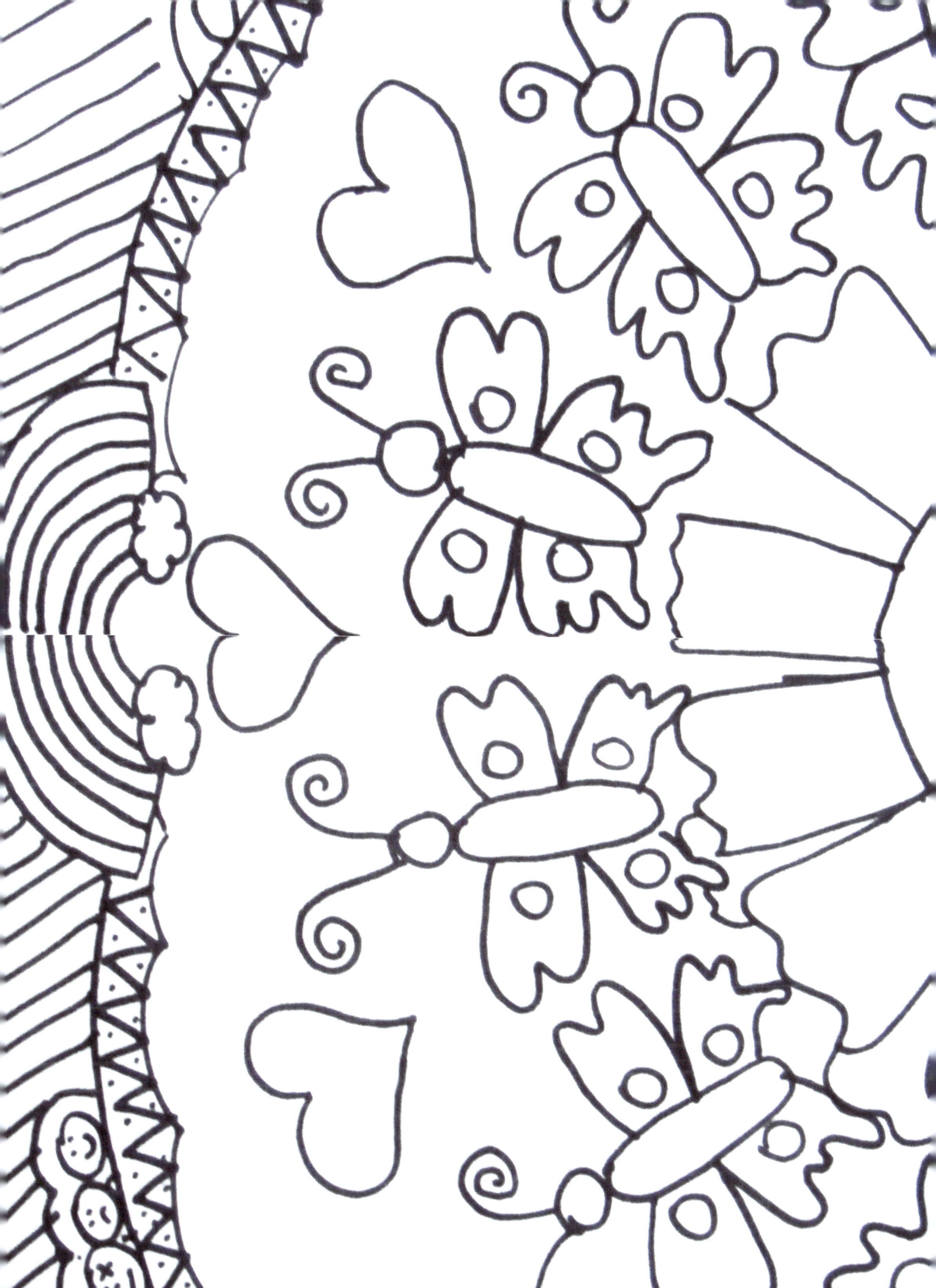

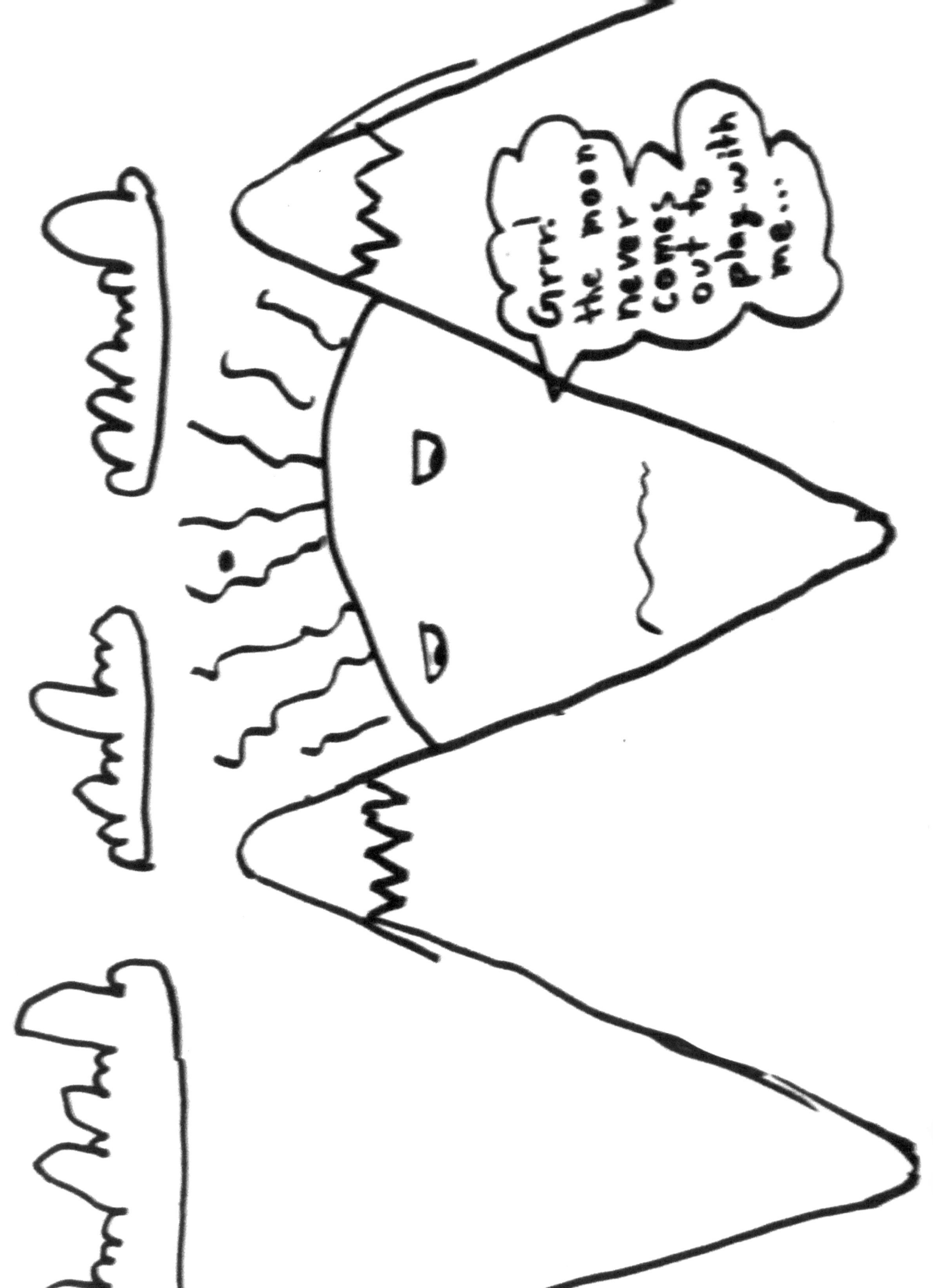

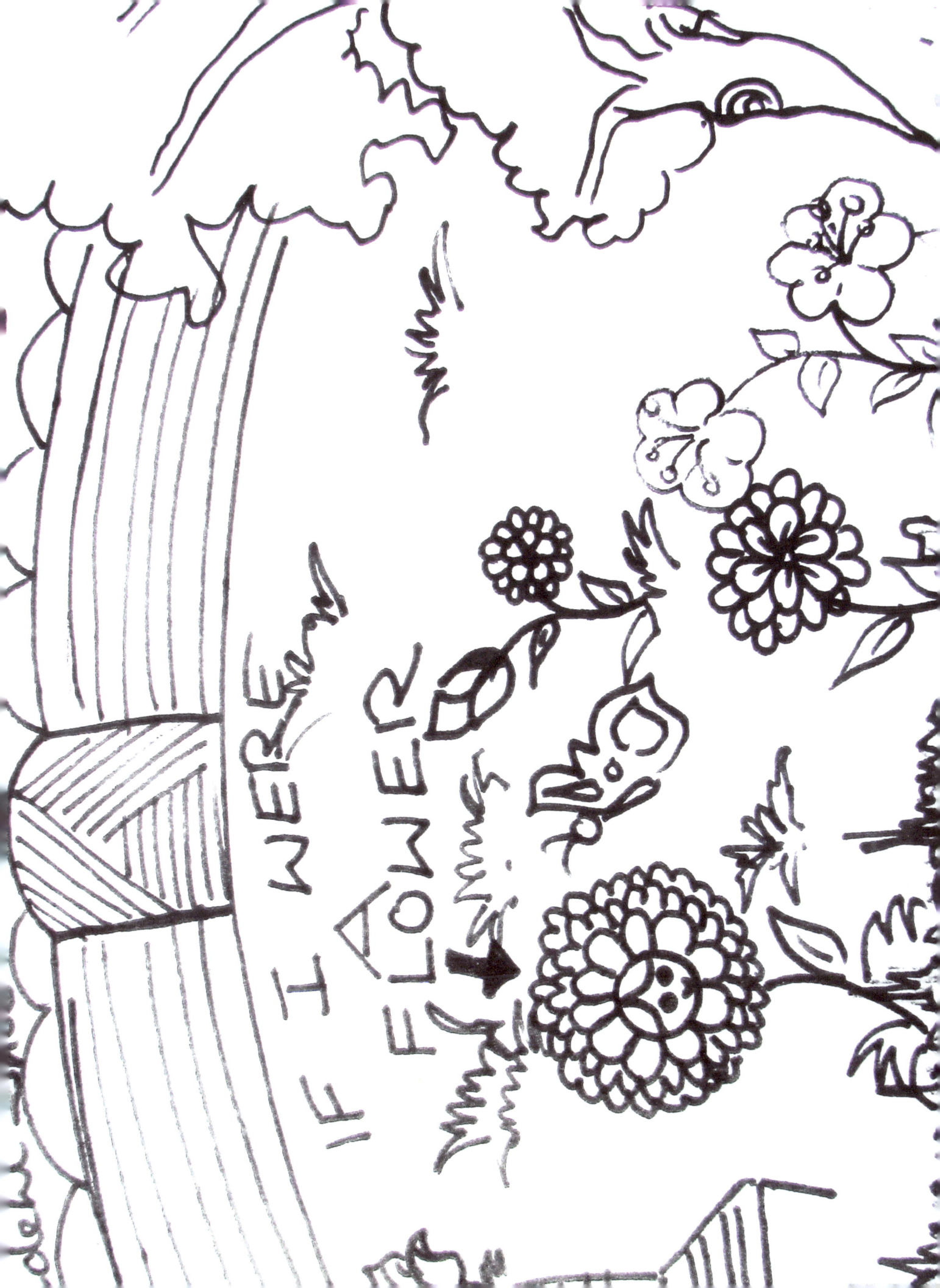

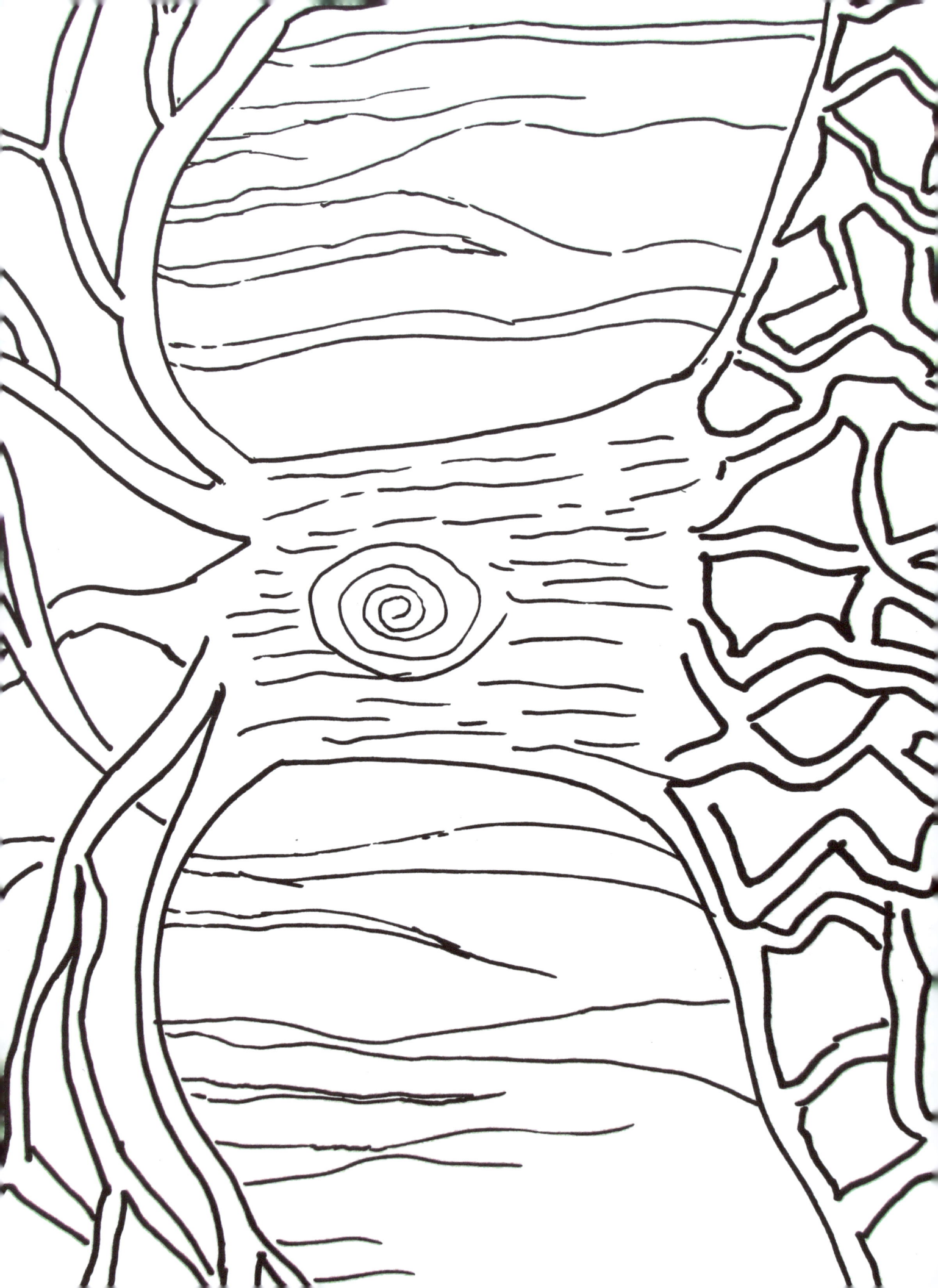

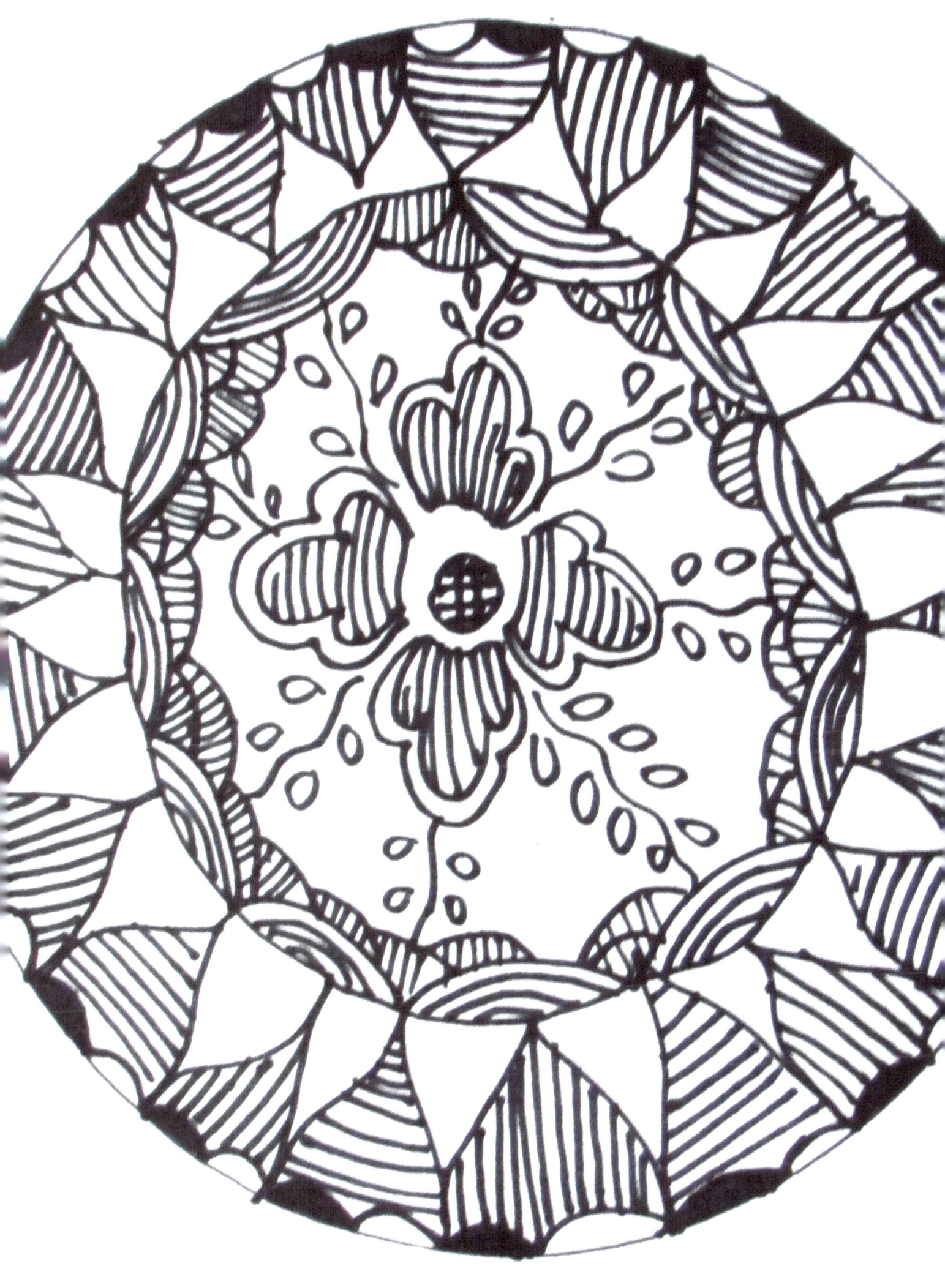

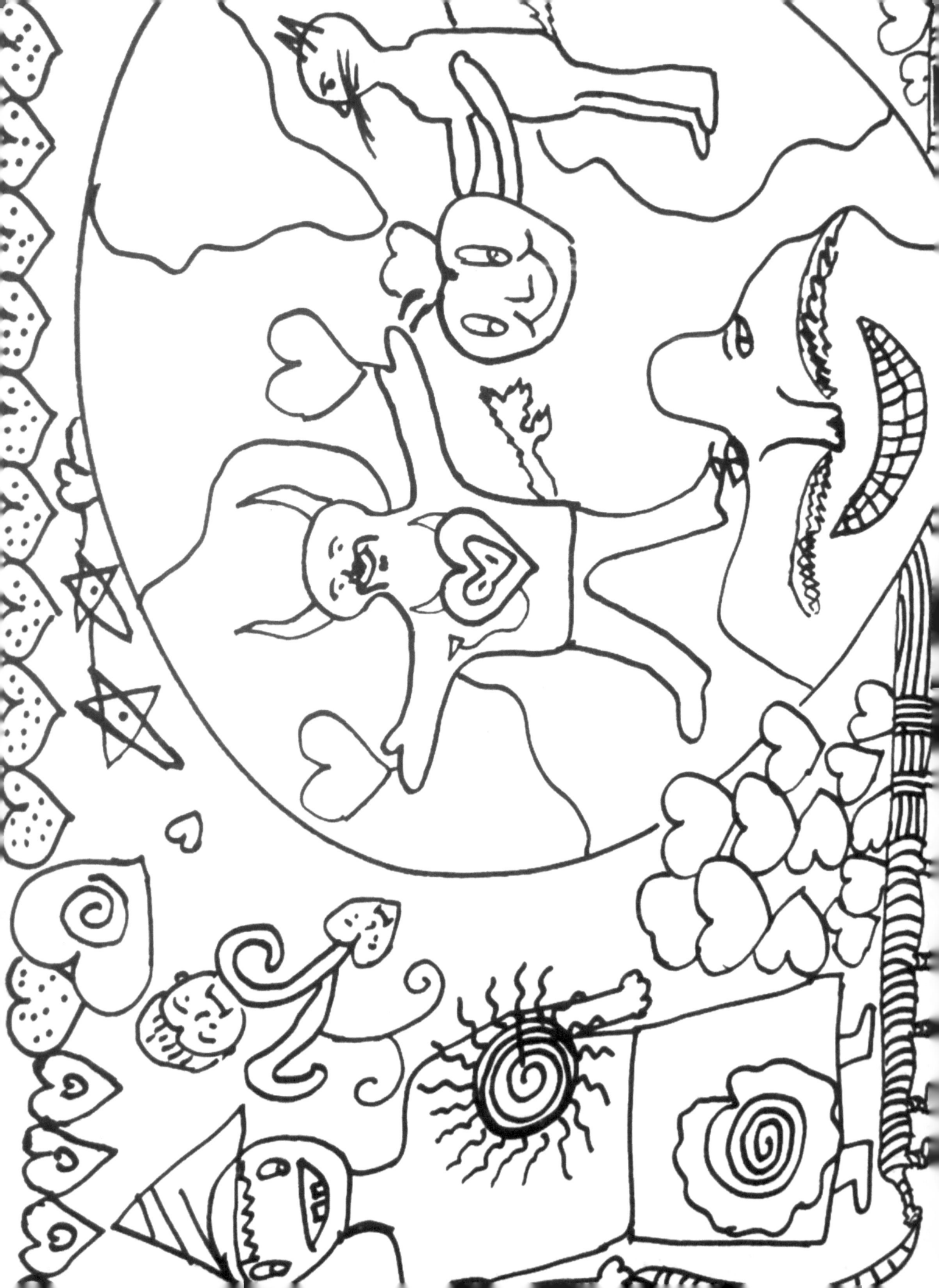

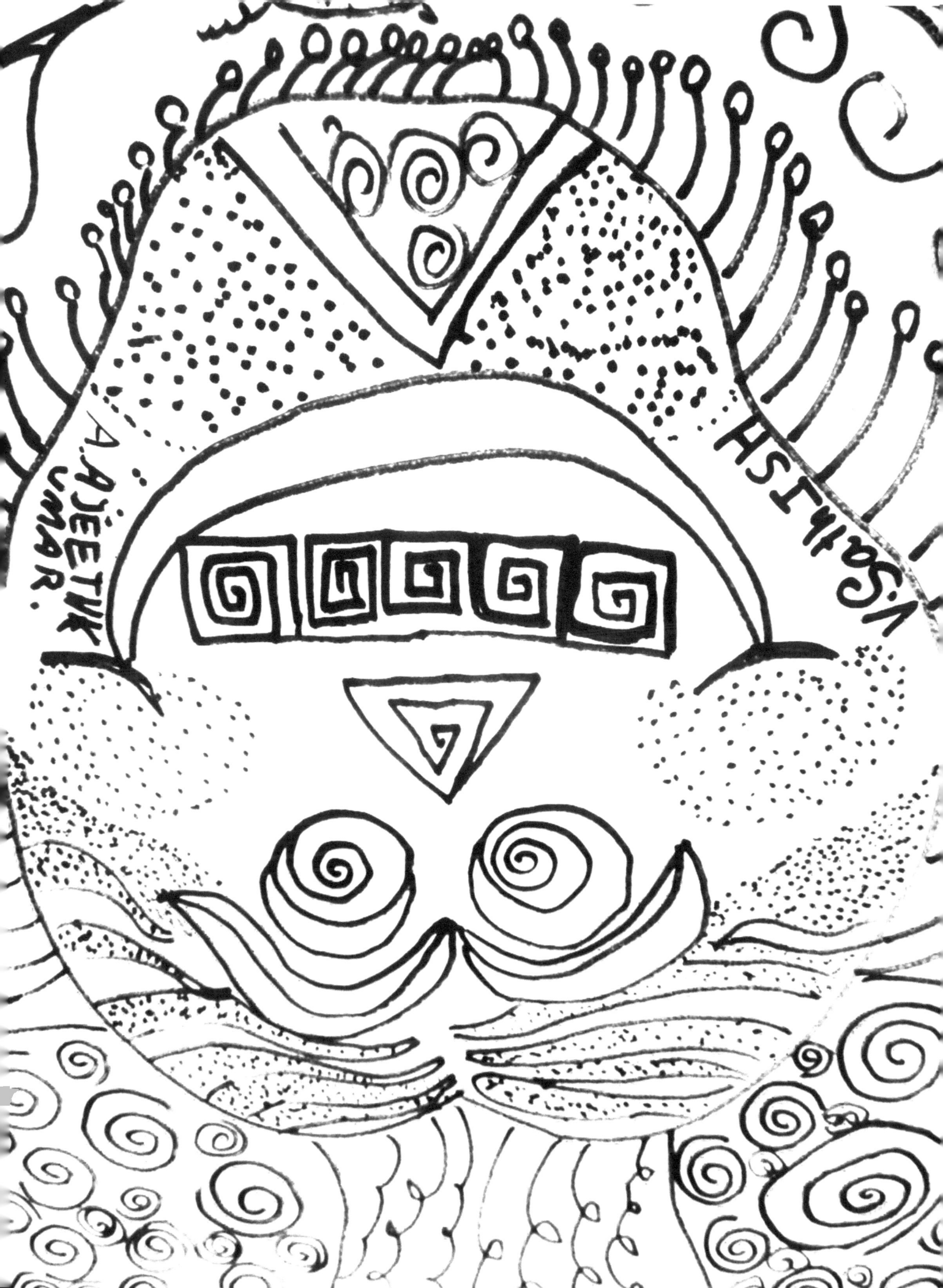

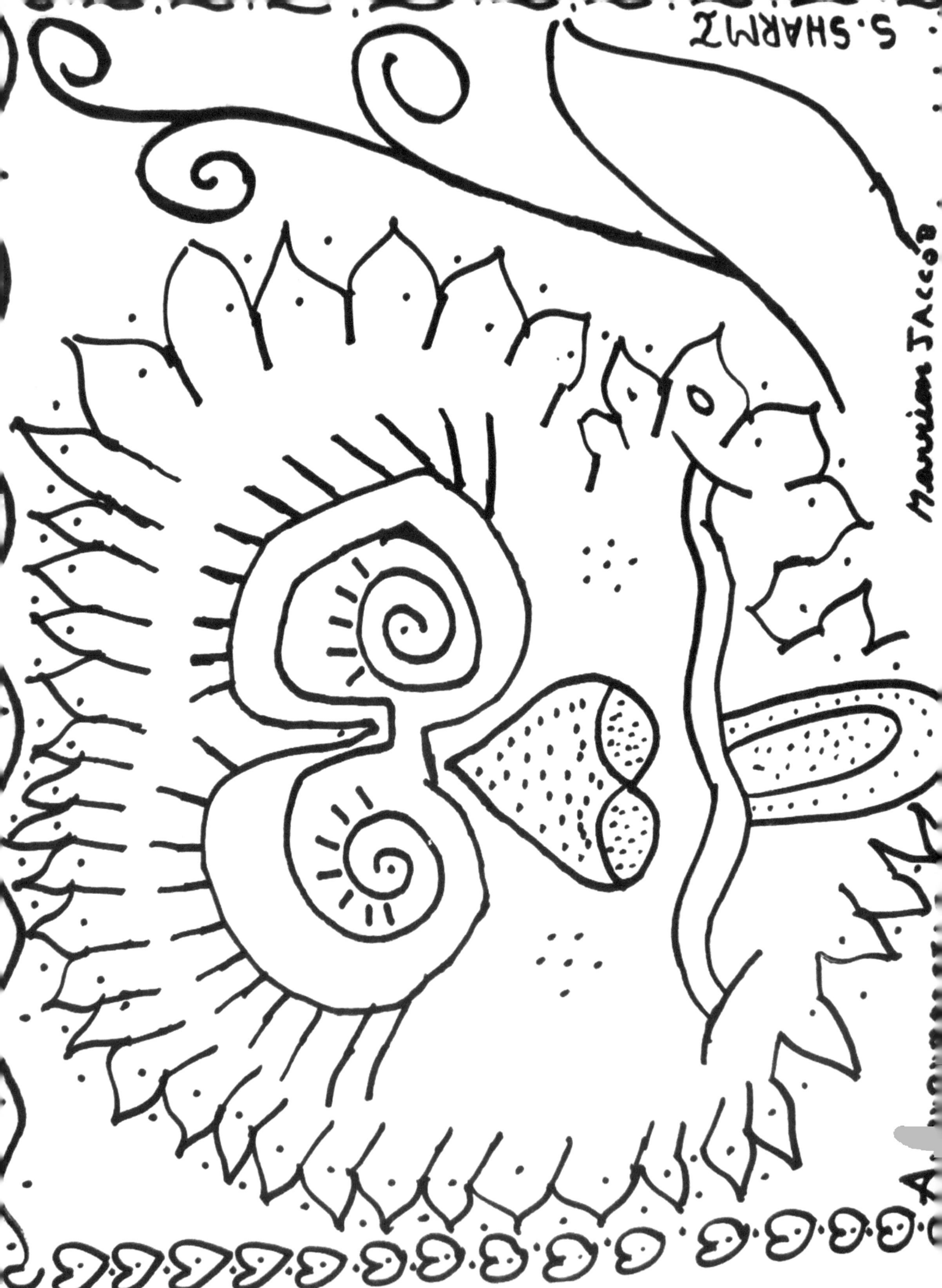

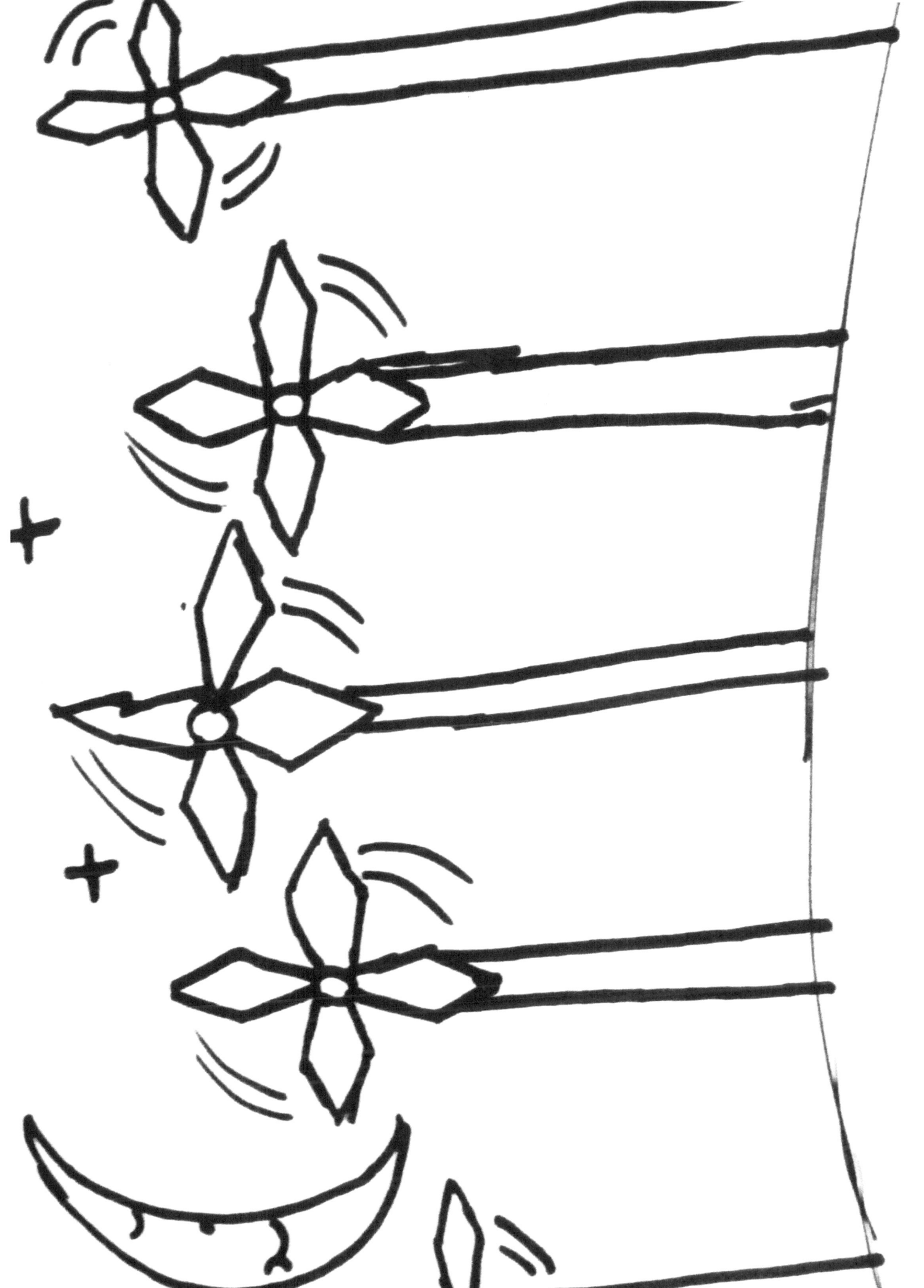

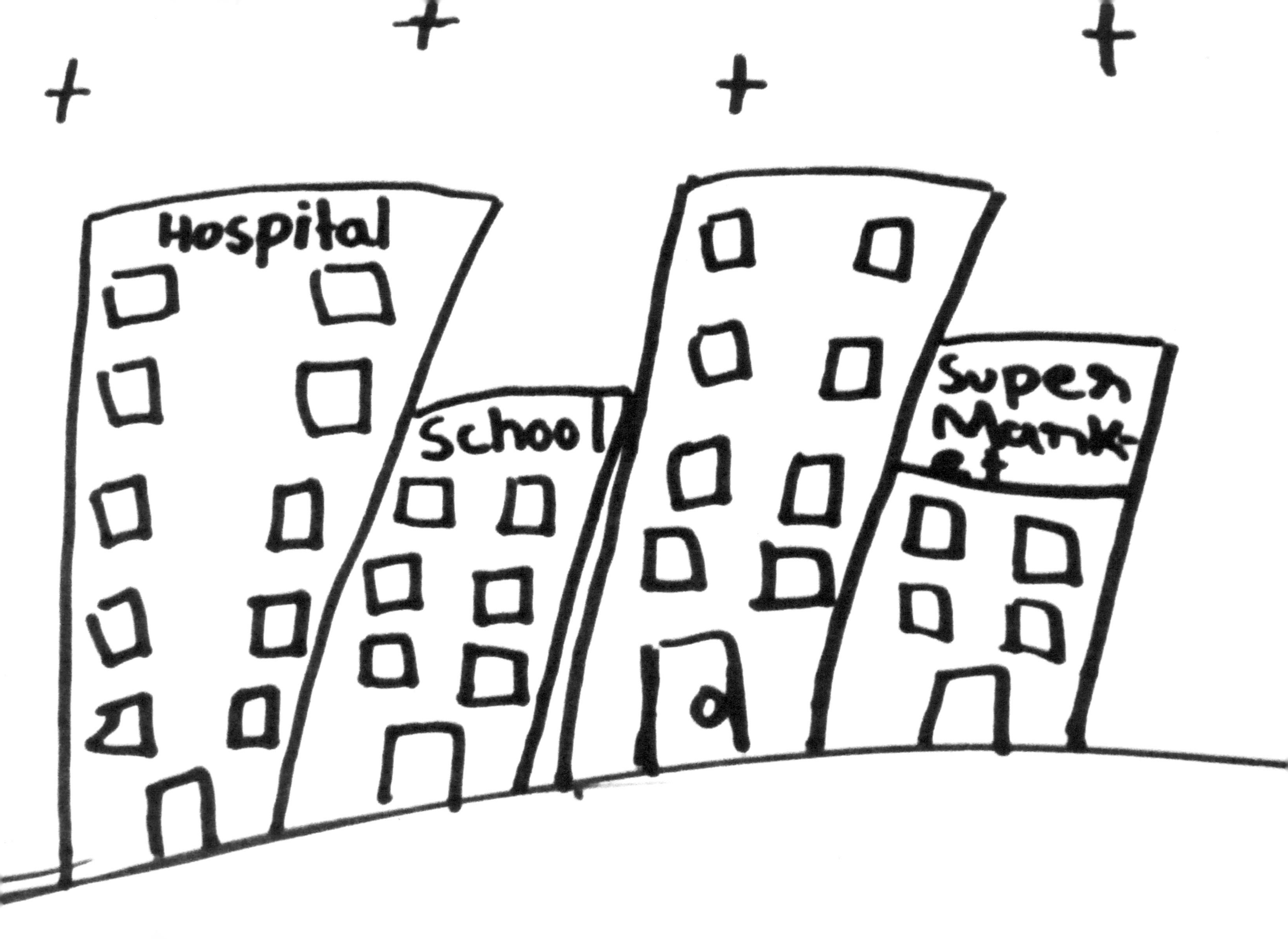
Hospital
School

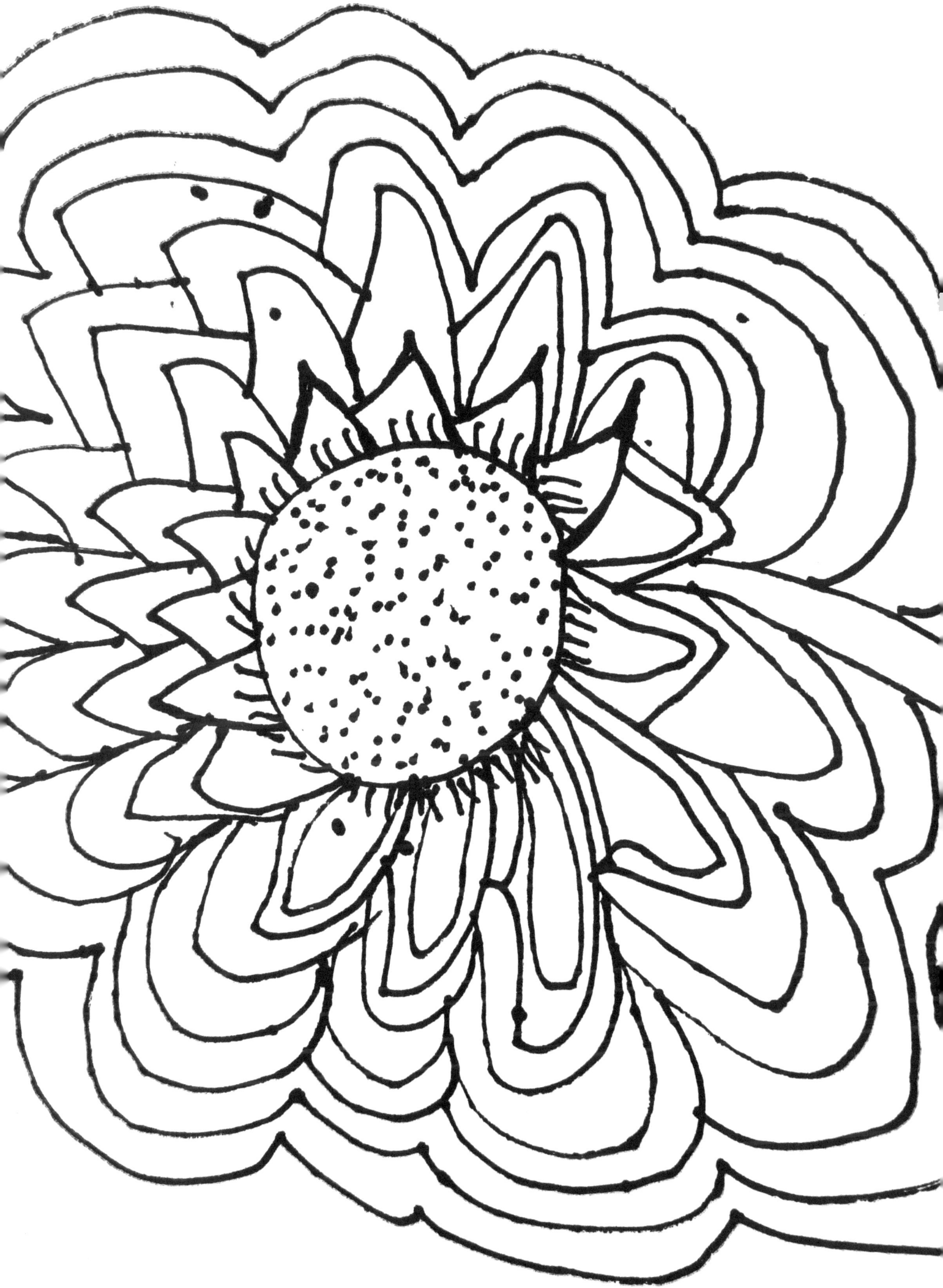

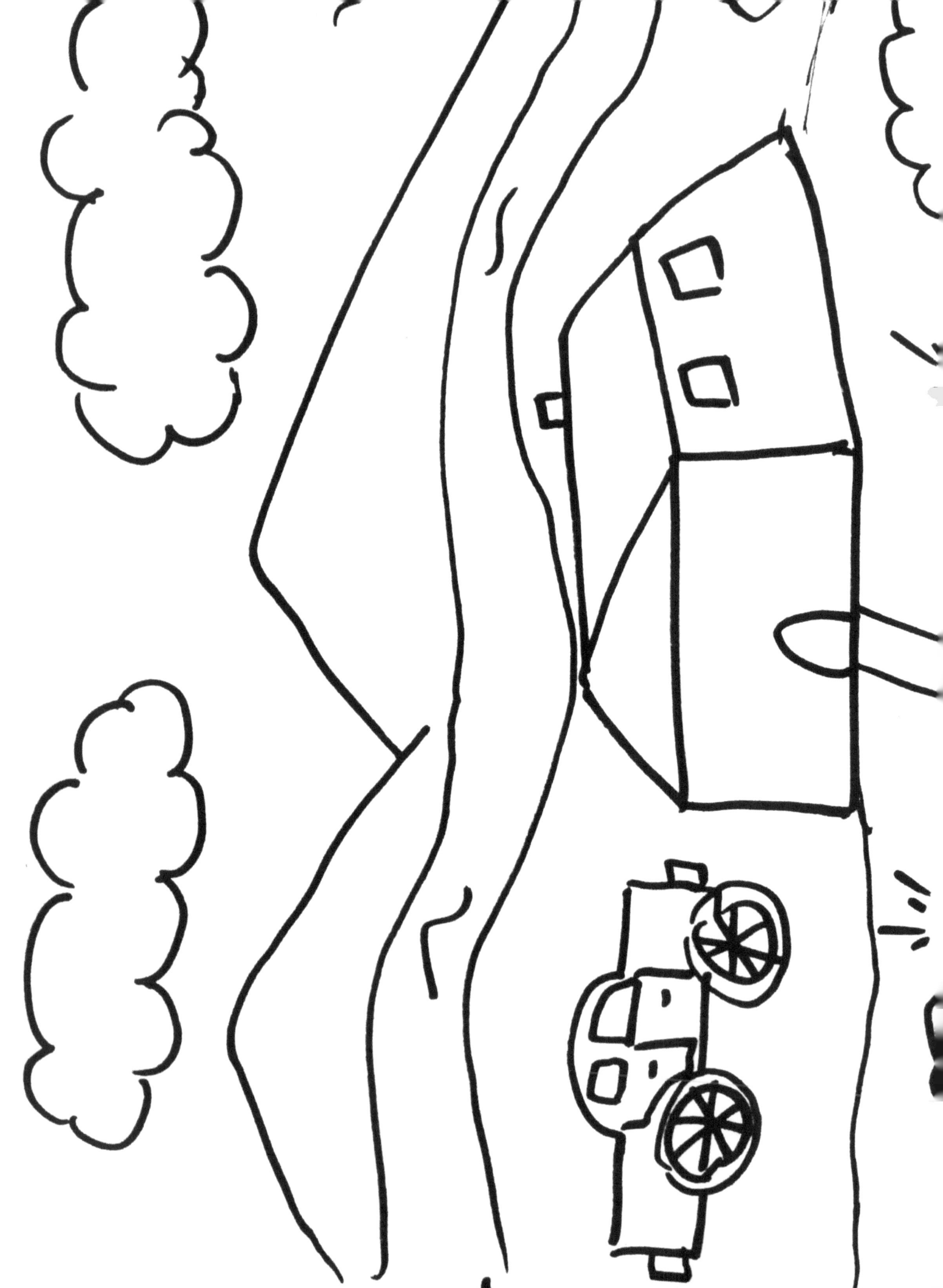

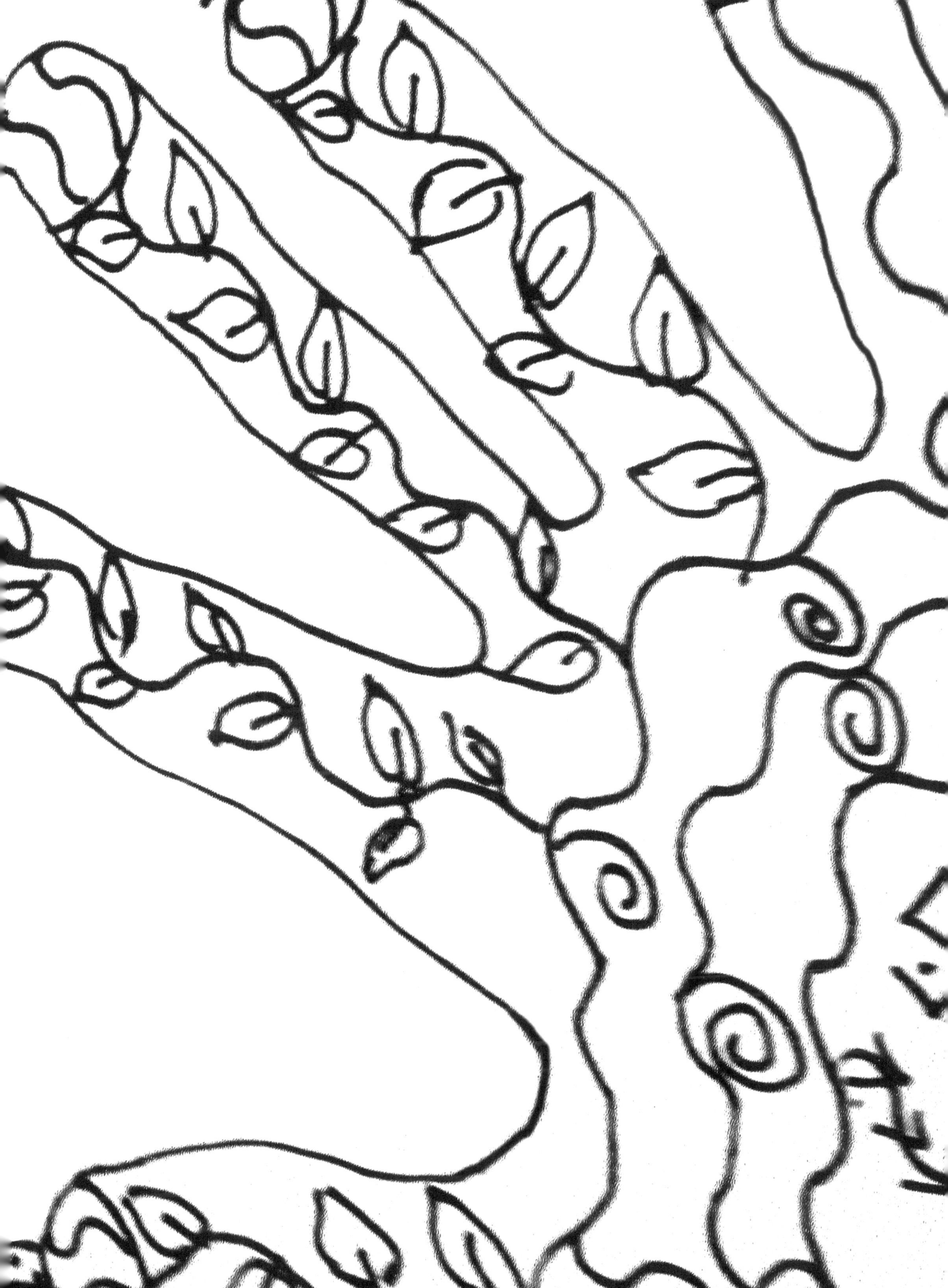

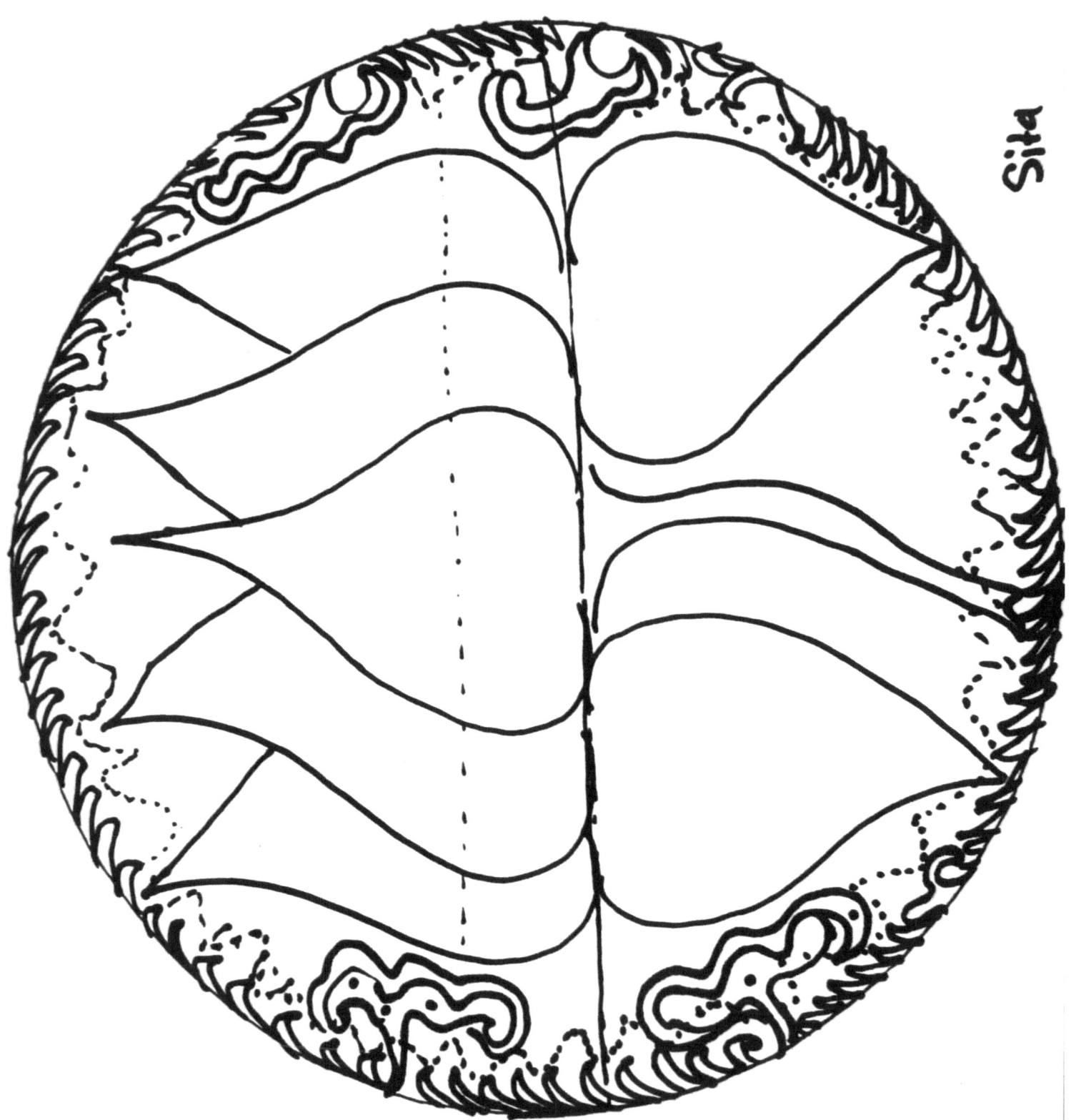

Sita

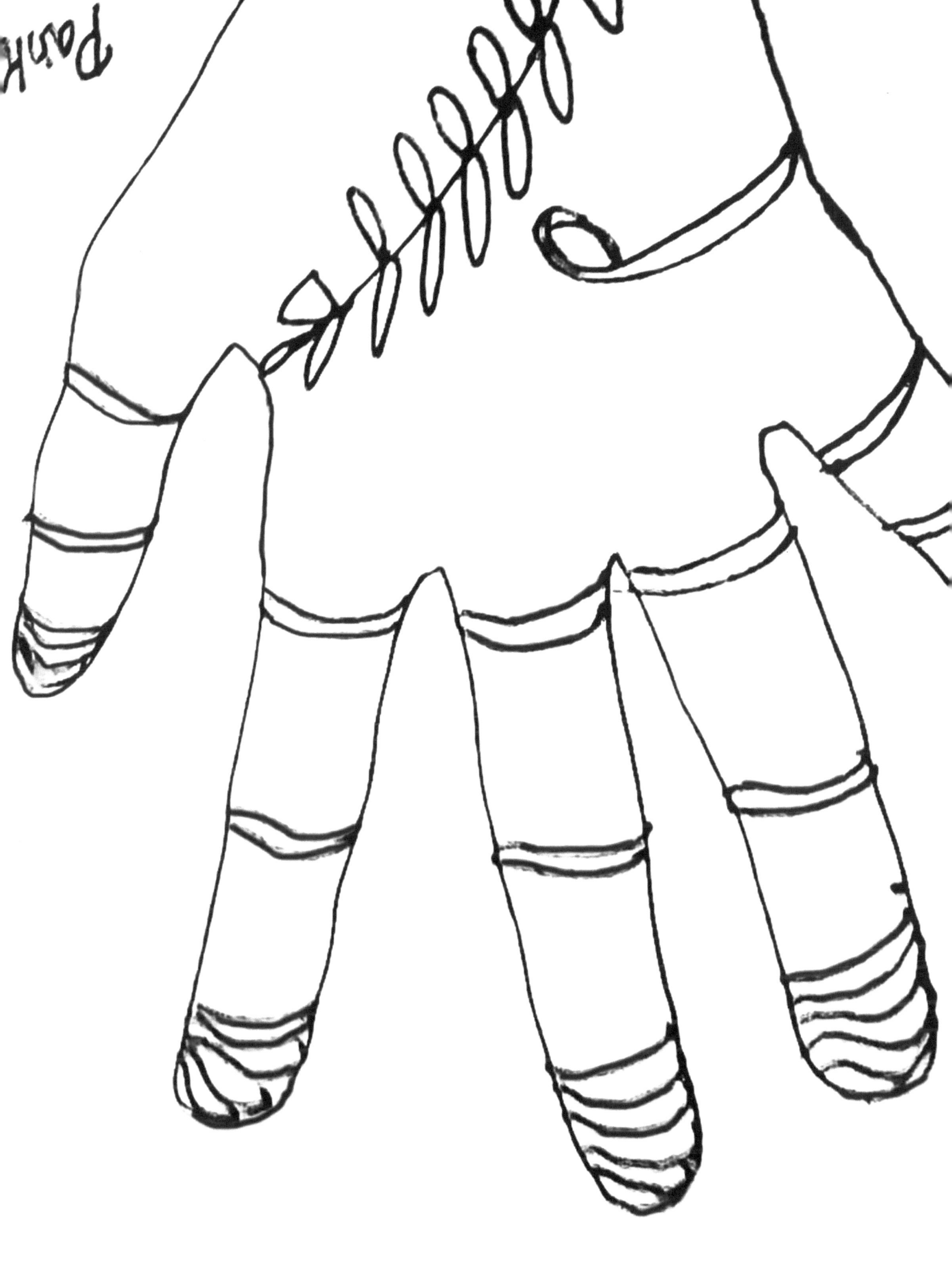

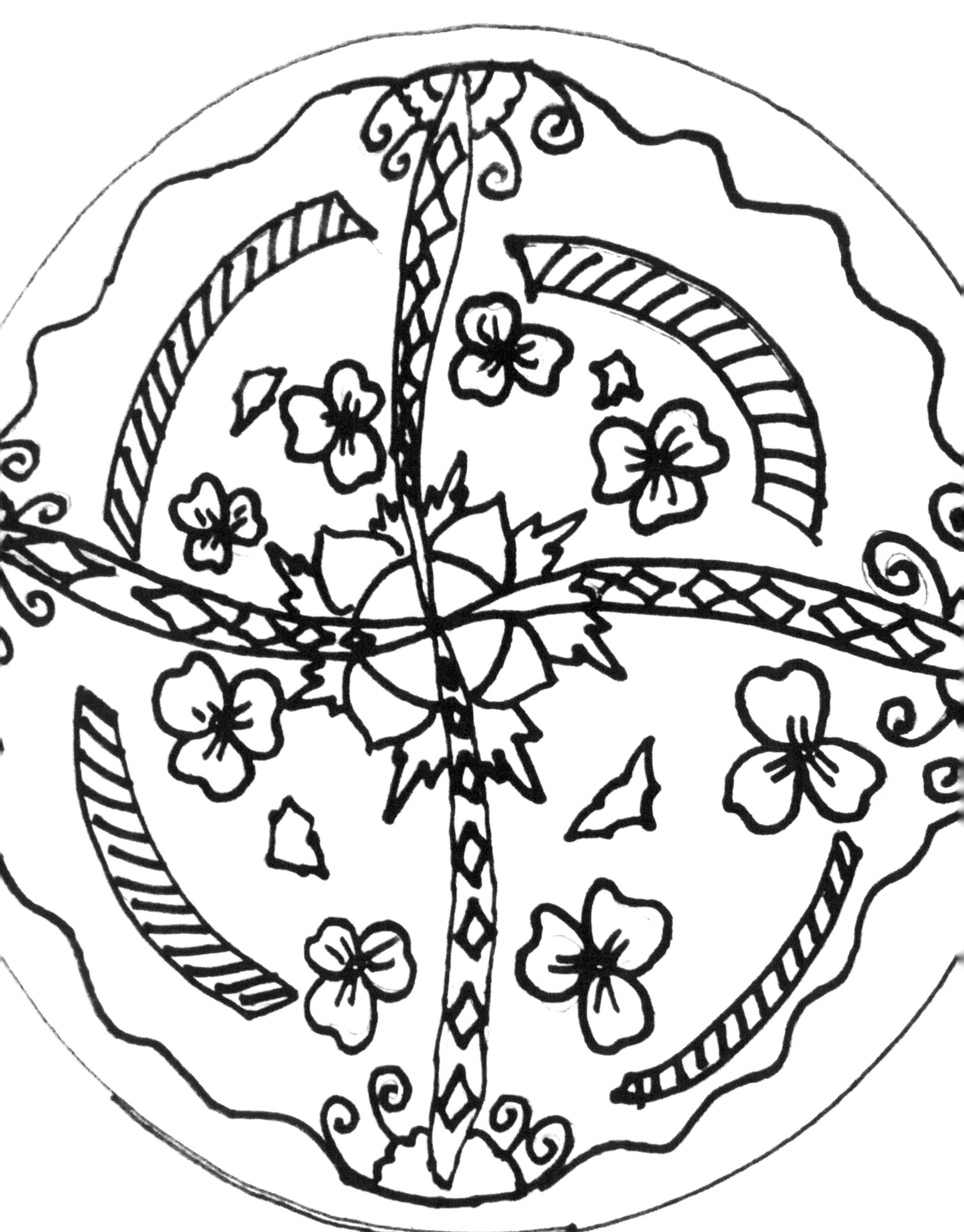

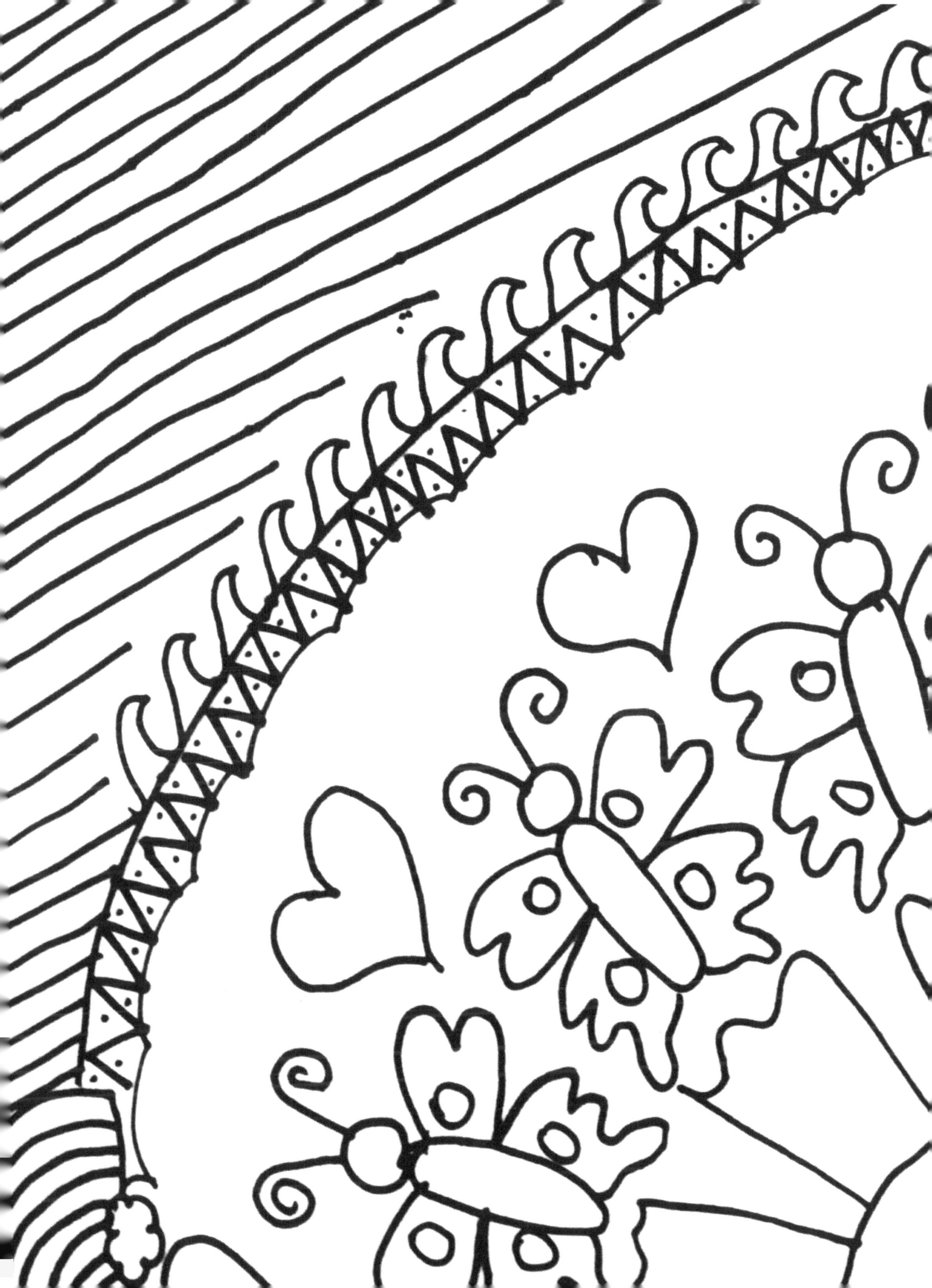

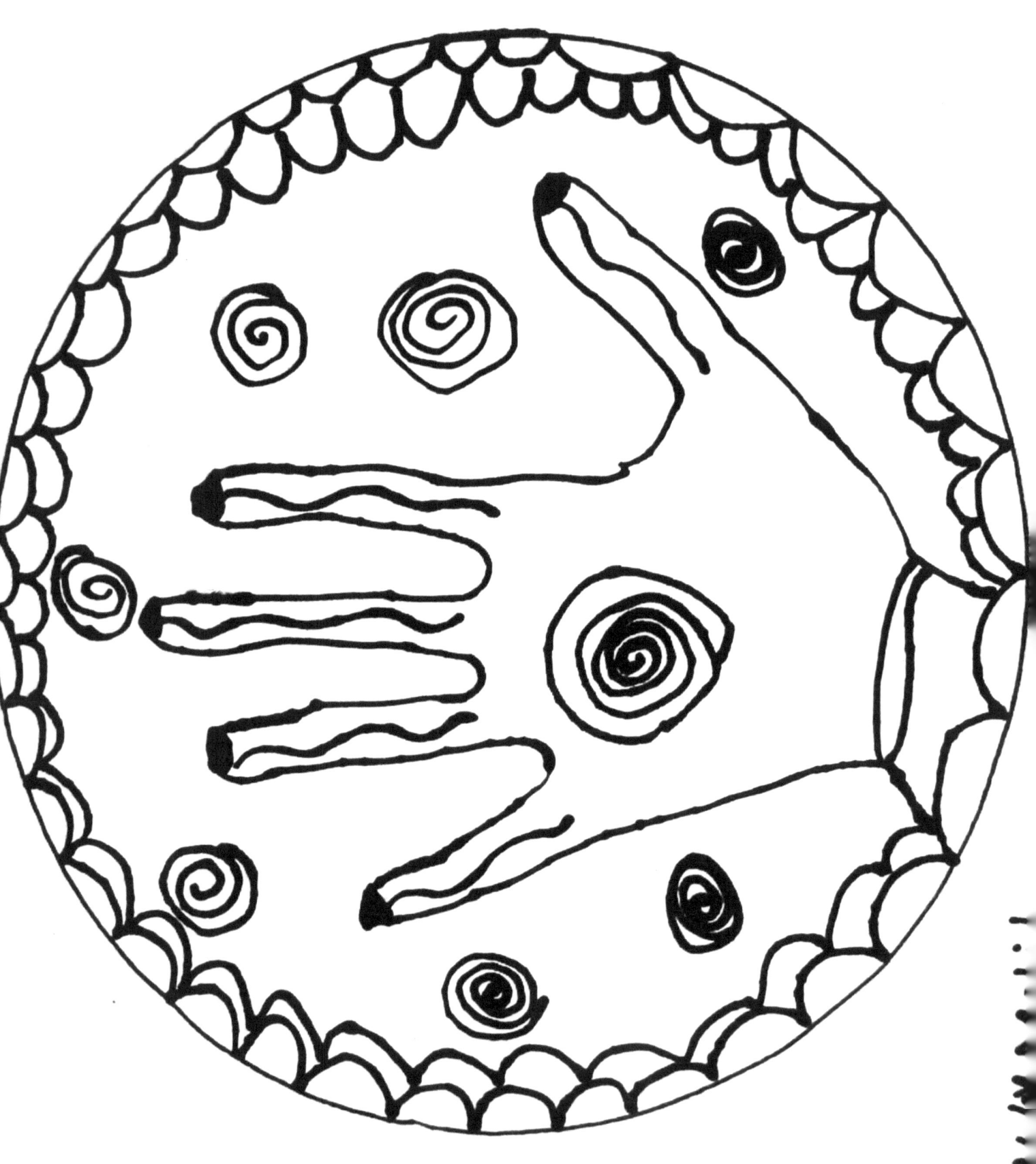

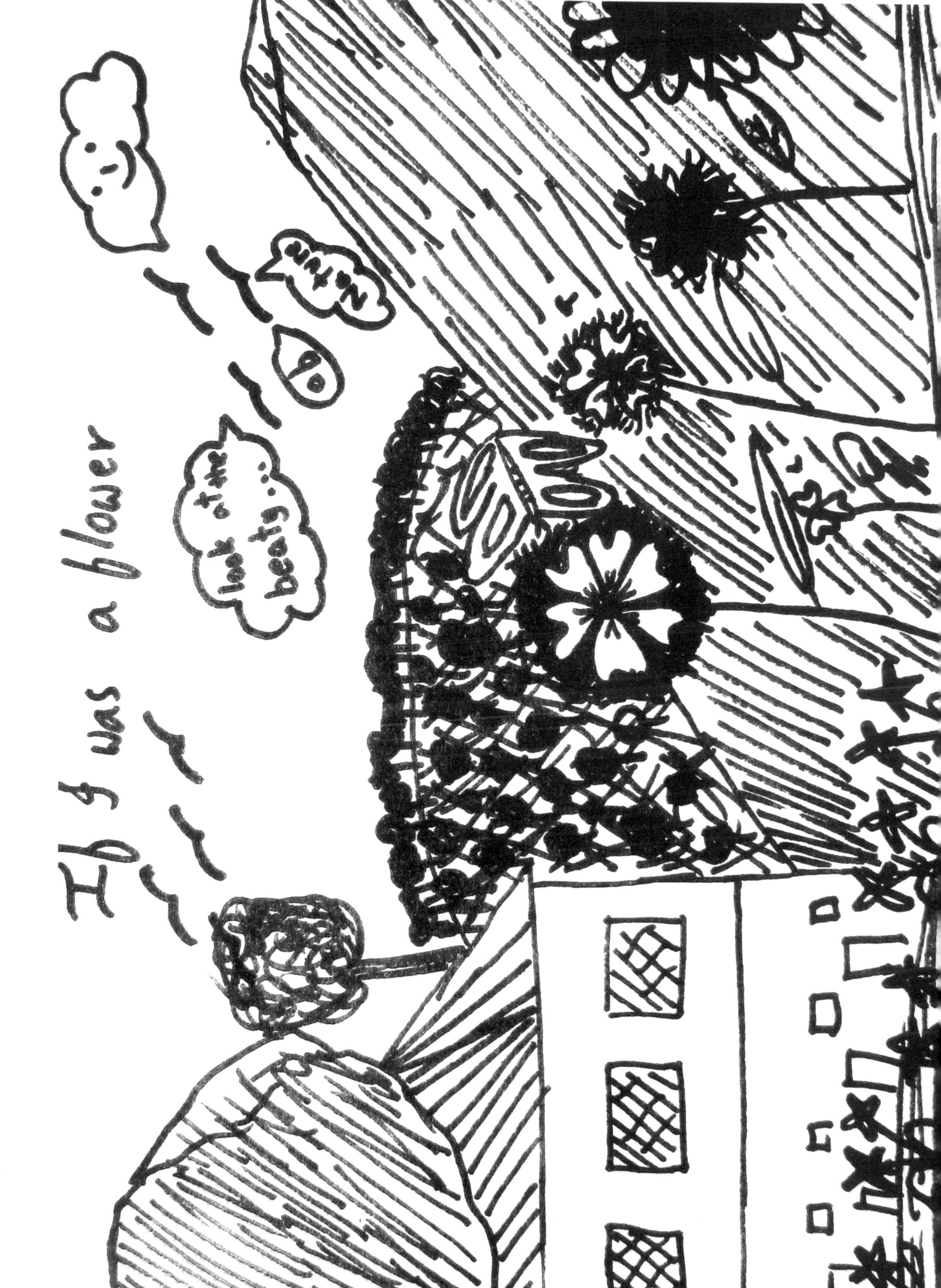

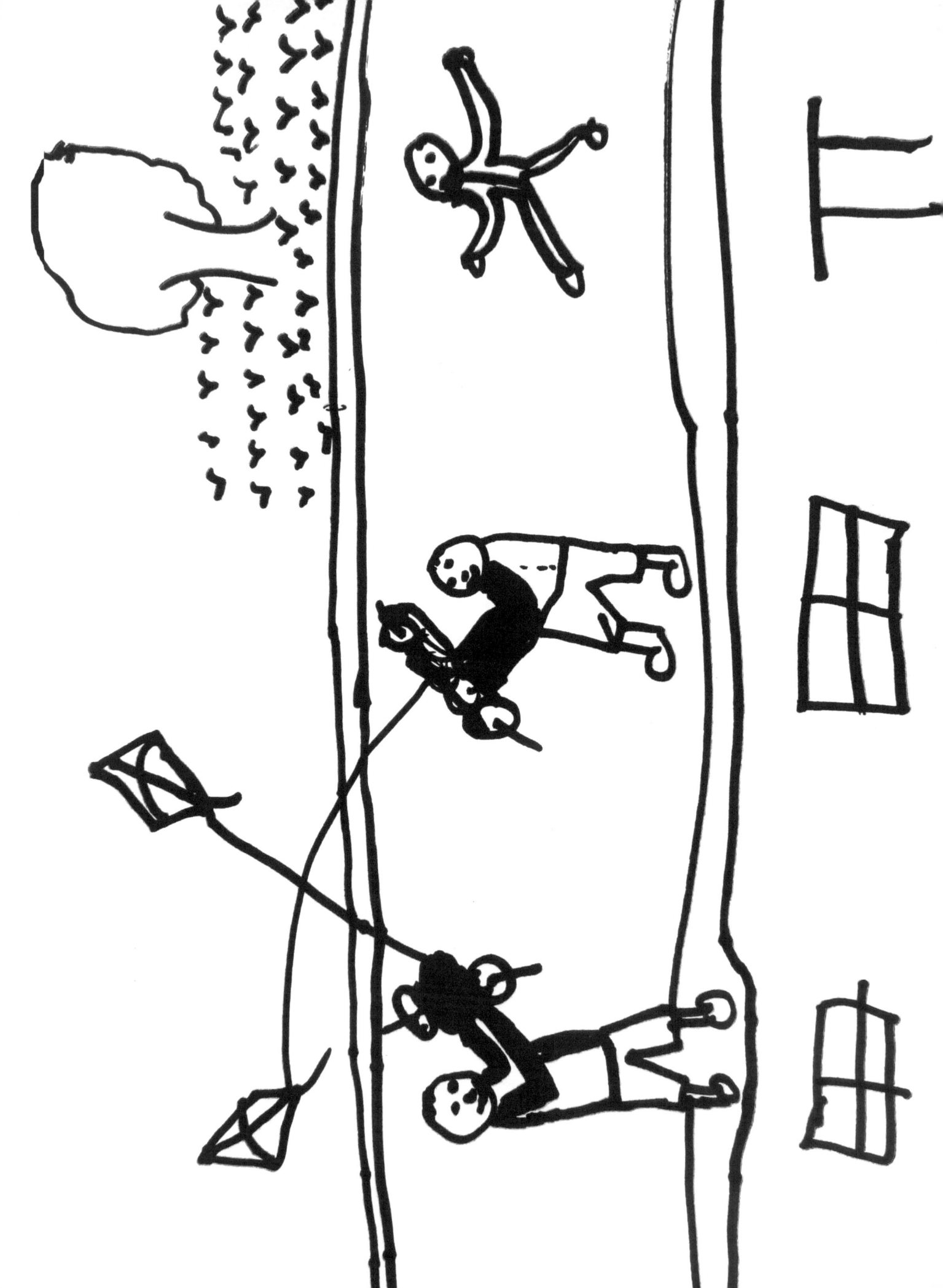

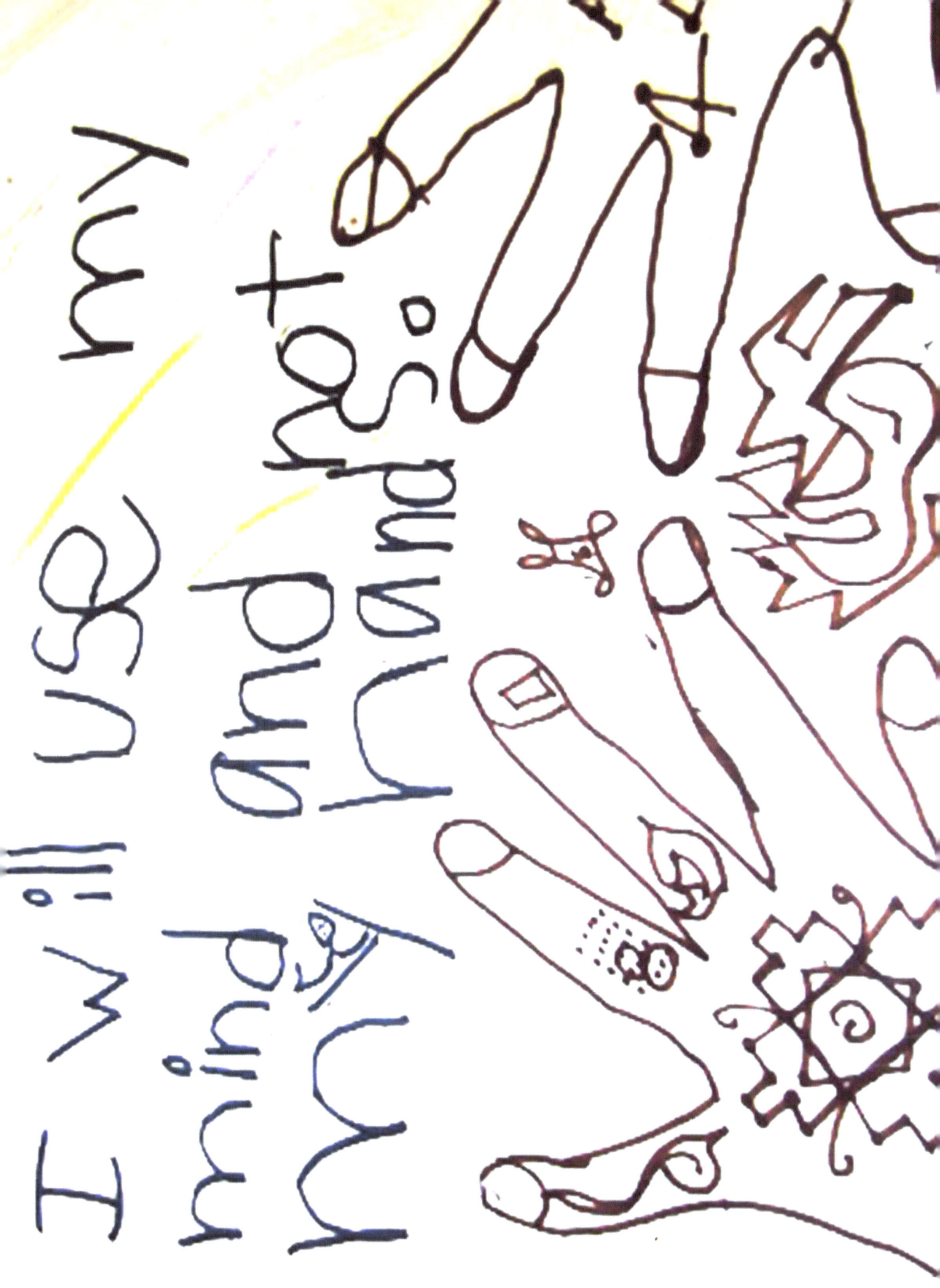

I will use my mind and my hands to make and plant

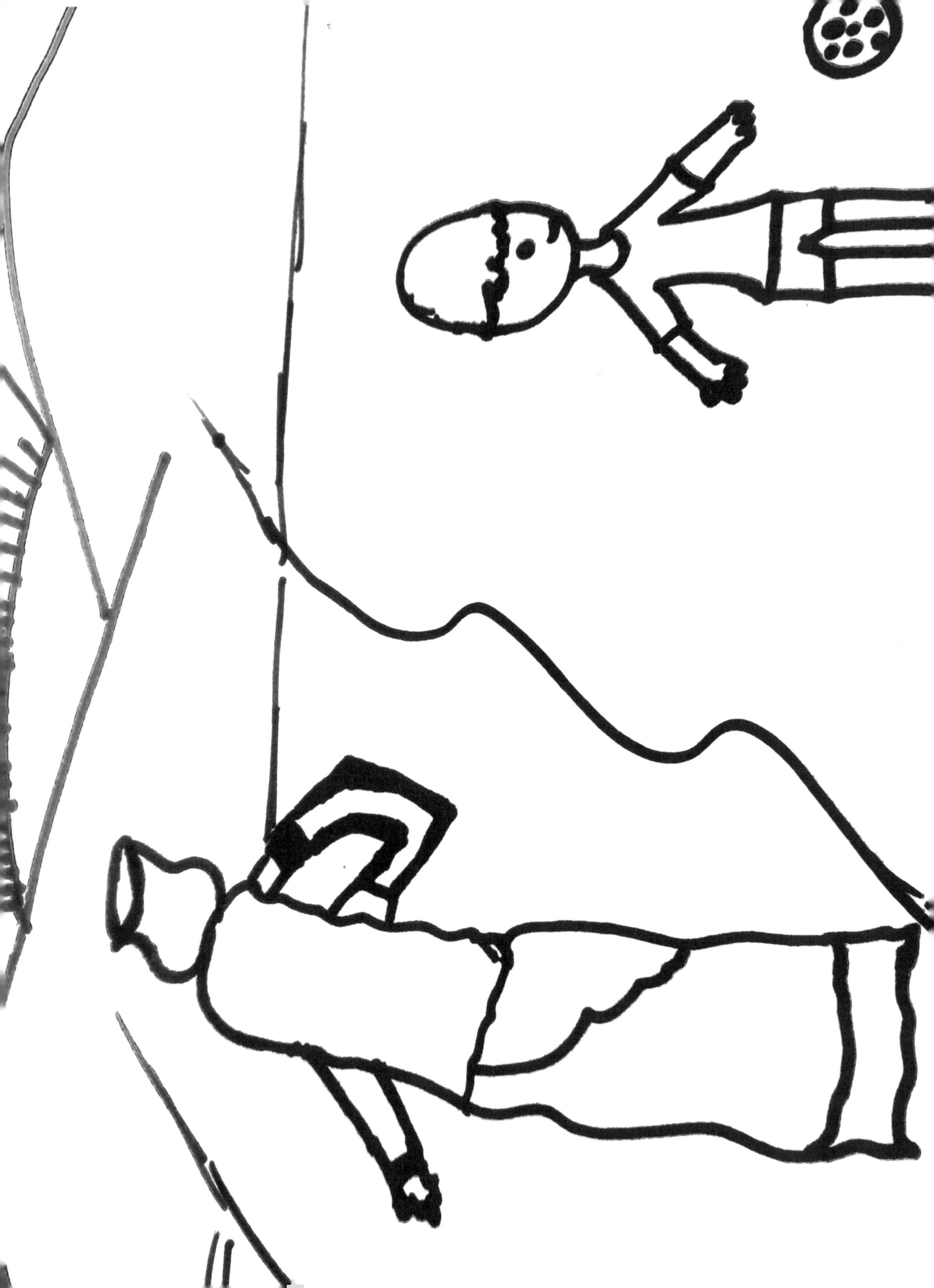

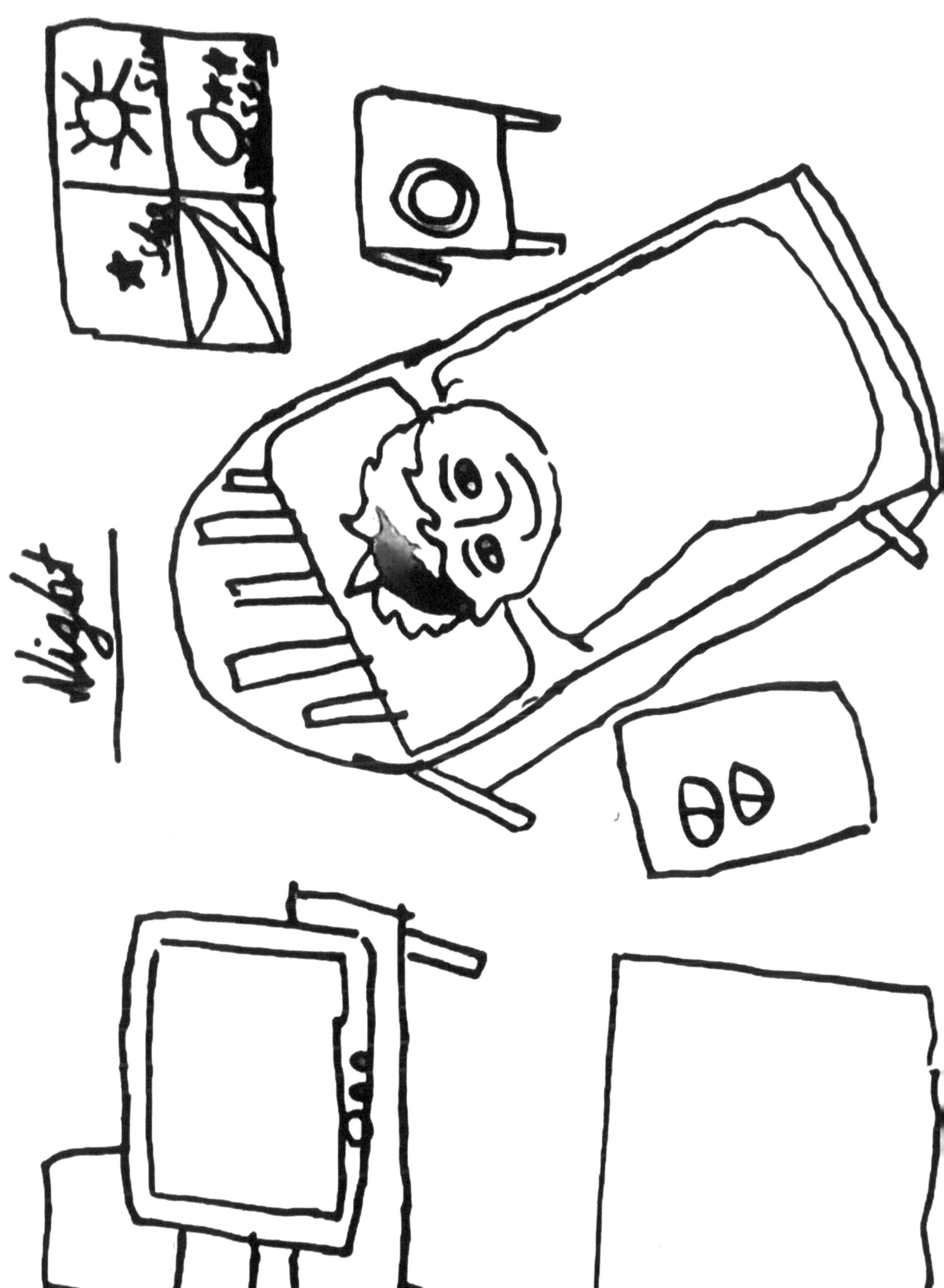

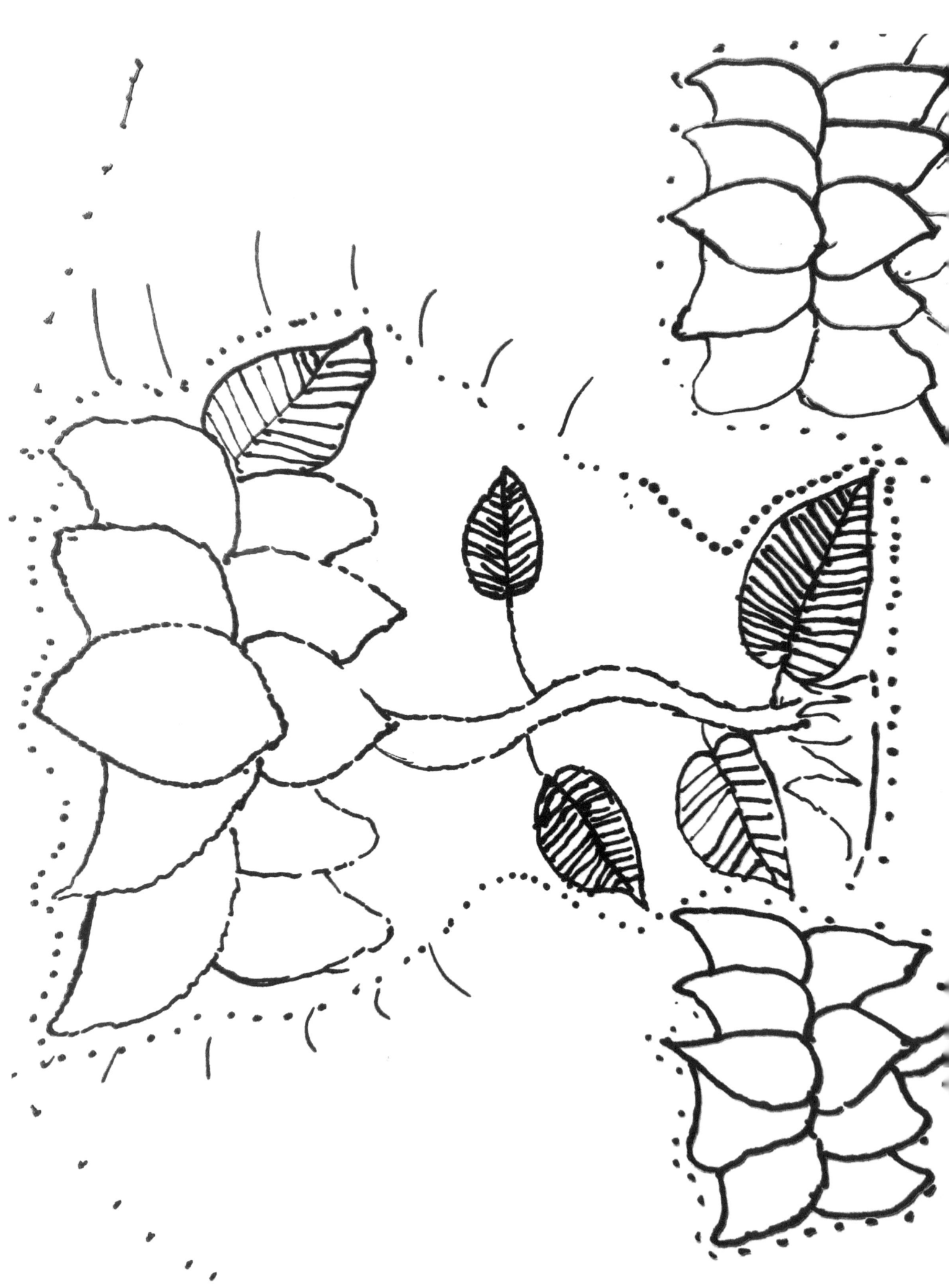

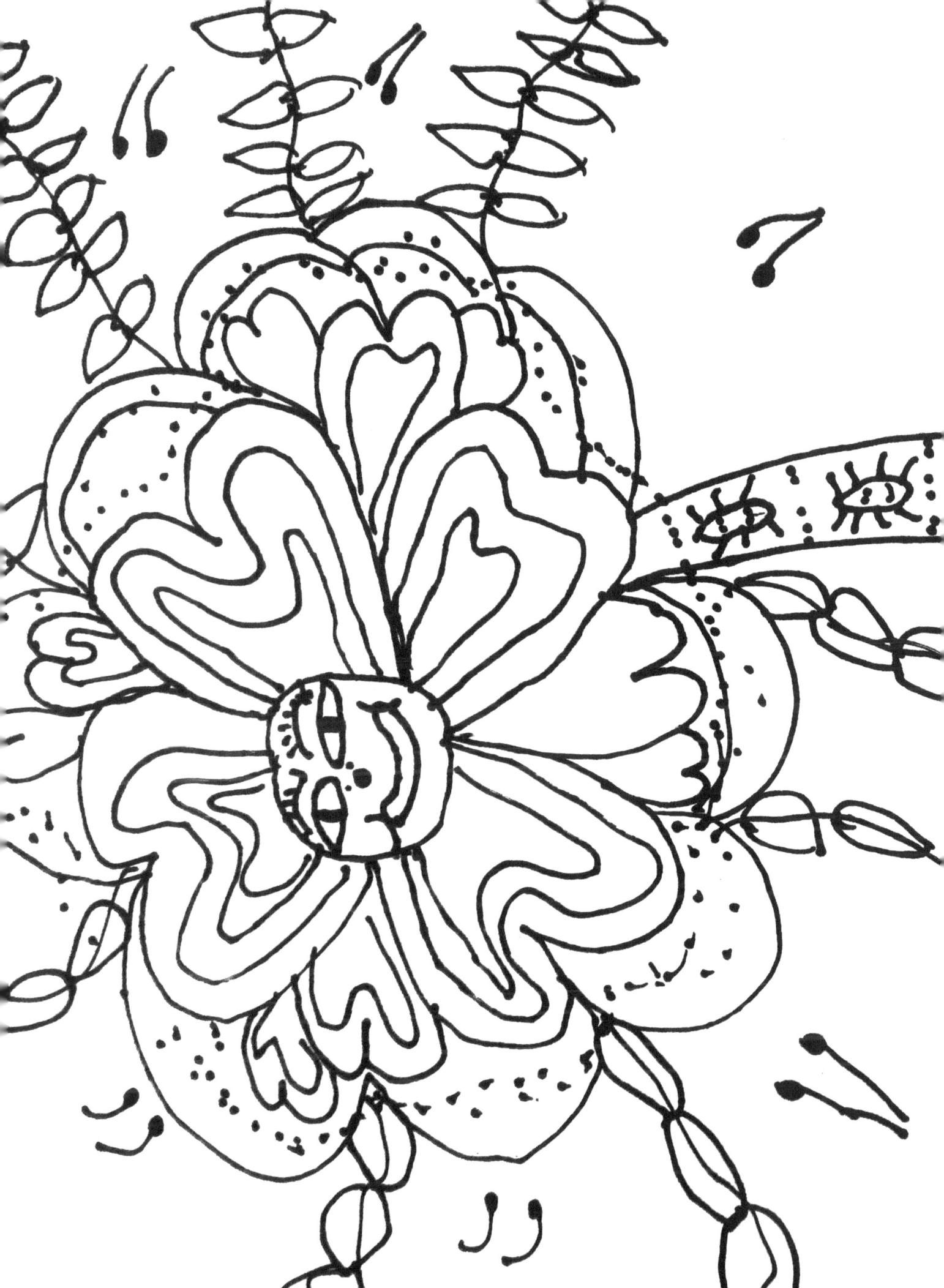

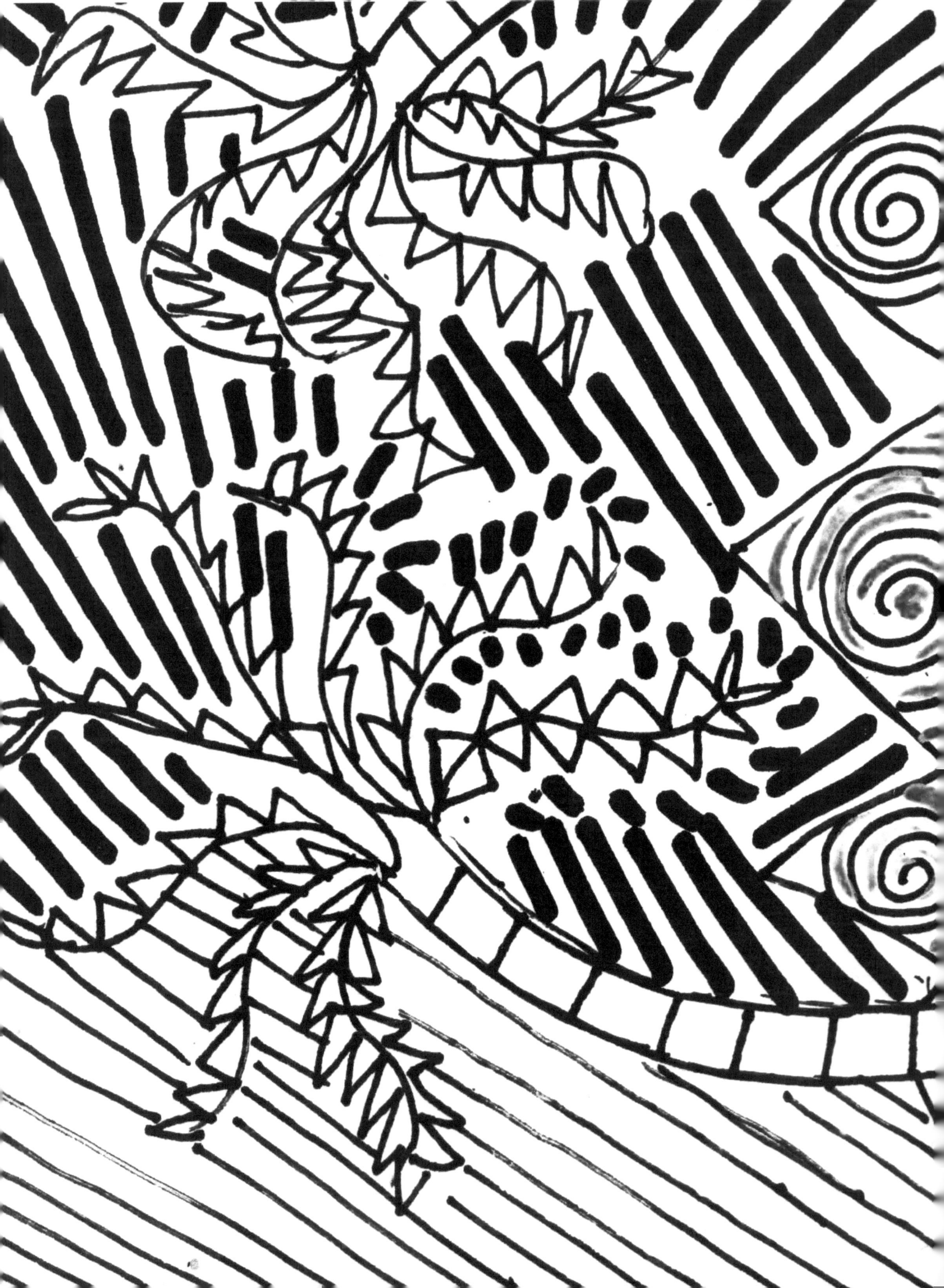

Acknowledgements

I would like to thank, with deep, heart-felt appreciation and gratitude…

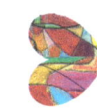 The students, teachers and Principal of Aikiyam School, Kuilapalayam, Auroville, South India…. for the support and freedom provided to me and for the infinite creativity, boundless energy and imagination displayed by all the village children…. especially, the first time authors and artists. Creating books by kids for kids was their idea, specifically of two young boys, who wanted to create an ABC Book for the youngest children to learn the alphabet. This is where Integral Art and Literacy came together to give birth to this wonderful project.

 The Sri Aurobindo Ashram, Delhi Branch, New Delhi, India and Madhuban, Uttarakhand, North India whose Village Outreach program enabled me to guide and inspire both students and teachers according to the philosophy and practices of Integral Art (Integral Education and Art Therapy), in addition to providing the art space and materials that has enabled Village Voices to continue blooming.

 The students, teachers and Principal of Sunrise Public School in Talla Ramgarh Uttarakhand…whose appreciation for art, creativity and the enhancement of social, emotional and intellectual development was always expressed with great enthusiasm and joy.

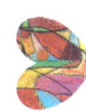 Indira Ranamagar , Amanda McKay and the children of Firefly Children's Home / PA Nepal (Prisoners Assistance Nepal) Sankhu, Kathmandu, Nepal… Opened their arms and their hearts for my program and projects. www.panepal.org

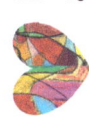 Foundation for World Education… through funds provided by a grant which supports Integral Education, awarded to the Sri Aurobindo Ashram Delhi Branch, graphic design work on four Village Voices books was able to begin, in order to prepare for publishing.

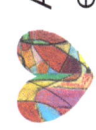 Anthea Guinness of Salt River Publishing who upon her very first and only encounter with Village Voices, embraced the project with open arms and a huge heart and provided fresh ideas, design, expansions and directions…www.saltriverpublishing.com

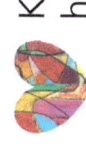 Kartik Gera, graphic designer who is passionate about Children's Literature, is a pleasure to work with and has the patience to deal with my lack of technological skills.

BREAK THE TREND

A London publisher once said, "People will beg, borrow or steal a book, but not buy."

Choose to be a buyer! Don't lend your copy to all your friends – order two copies of this book **today** and give them away.

This is your chance to stand with all of us – the writers, artists, editors and designers associated with the no-profit Salt River Publishing company.

www.SaltRiverPublishing.com
Publisher discount available at the estore

SALT RIVER

Salt River Publishing believes in encouraging artists and publishing professionals to come together and reach their empowered "Yes!"

Salt River was established as a no-profit publisher with the idea of helping writers, translators, poets, graphic artists and photographers bring their work into publishable form.

We provide links to a range of publishing professionals who offer services for anybody with a book in the making.

And we publish books that inspire, encourage and entertain, including children's books and books that deepen the understanding of mysticism.

Do you have one?

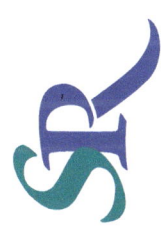

www.SaltRiverPublishing.com

READER RESPONSE
TO SALT RIVER BOOKS

"So many problems are spiritual in nature. And healing often involves finding meaning, purpose and spiritual uplift. The right words at the right time can turn a life around. Therapists and practitioners can point the way for clients who are seeking meaning; writers and artists have an opportunity to share in that work. Thank you, Salt River."